ECHOING
GOD'S LOVE

A CONTEMPORARY
COLLECTION OF INSPIRATIONAL STORIES

ECHOING
GOD'S LOVE

Charles Mills

REVIEW AND HERALD® PUBLISHING ASSOCIATION
HAGERSTOWN, MD 21740

The author assumes full responsibility for the accuracy of all facts and quotations as cited in this book.

Texts credited to NIV are from the *Holy Bible, New International Version.* Copyright © 1973, 1978, 1984, International Bible Society. Used by permission of Zondervan Bible Publishers.

This book was
Edited by Gerald Wheeler
Copyedited by James Cavil
Designed by Patricia S. Wegh
Cover photo by Tony Stone Images
Interior illustrations by Denny Bond
Typeset: 11/15 Bembo

PRINTED IN U.S.A.

03 02 01 00 99   5 4 3 2 1

R&H Cataloging Service
Mills, Charles Henning, 1950-
        Echoing God's love.

            1. Christian life.   2. Religious life.   I. Title.
                        248.4

ISBN 0-8280-1326-8

DEDICATION

In loving memory
of my mother,
El Rita Mills,
who spent
her entire life
echoing God's love
to me.

ABOUT THE AUTHOR

Four months after Charles Mills was born, General Douglas MacArthur blew up his house. Charles says he's always tried not to take that personally. The Korean War sent missionaries of all faiths running for cover, including the Mills family, who escaped Japan before moving on to the Philippines and Singapore.

Charles grew up in a household dedicated to biblical ideals. His father, a treasurer and administrator for a wide range of Christian institutions, led the family around the world, serving in the Far East, North America, and the Middle East. The missionary flame burned brightly in Charles even after he left the family fold and headed for Southern Missionary College, in Tennessee. During his junior year he took a break from his studies in broadcast communications and spent a year in Japan, teaching English at an evangelistic center in Osaka. After graduating in 1973, Charles helped produce Christian television programs in southern California, managed a college radio station near San

Francisco, taught church school in Georgia, and formed his own media production company in Maryland and West Virginia. Along the way he earned a commercial pilot's license, taught flying from several small-town and metropolitan airports, and managed to marry Dorinda, a preacher's daughter, who he says "knows me and loves me anyway." Charles is also a prolific writer and musician.

"My number one goal in life," says Mills, "is to change people's concept of God. Many tend to view our heavenly Father as a stern judge messing up our lives in an attempt to lead us to salvation. That's not *my* God. He's the master of unmessing up lives by freely offering the salvation made possible by Christ's sacrifice."

When not writing manuscripts, creating videos and radio programs, or designing marketing materials for his clients, Charles enjoys bird watching, rummaging through antique malls, and making music on his keyboard and guitar.

Echoing God's Love is his thirtieth published book.

Contents

ECHOING GOD'S LOVE IN *HUMANITY*

HUMANITY

Recognizing God

He that hath seen me hath seen the Father. John 14:9.

A low fog bank hugged the waters as our big freighter sailed cautiously through the wide mouth of the harbor. I strained to see beyond the mists, but my 4-year-old eyes recognized nothing among the soft, liquid curtains.

It was my very first visit to America, having spent my entire life, short as it was, in eastern Asia, where my parents served as Christian missionaries. But it wasn't necessarily the United States that was the goal of my gaze that cold, damp morning. No, I was looking for an even more wondrous sight. I was looking for Grandma.

After all, I'd heard so much about her. My mom had told me stories of the kindhearted woman in whose care she'd grown up—stories of depression years when food was scarce but love wasn't, when Christmas presents had been handmade because the family had no extra money to spend. I knew in my little boy heart that somewhere beyond that fog bank waited a woman who'd love me just as she'd loved my mother. To me, Grandma and America were almost one and the same.

Suddenly, as our boat slipped through the glassy waters, I saw a figure begin to emerge from the mist. A tall, beautiful woman holding high a gleaming torch. "Mommy!" I cried, running along the damp, salty deck. "Mommy, there she is. There's Grandma!"

The image in my mind of a kindhearted woman waiting to welcome me to America fit perfectly the grand design of the Statue of Liberty. The sight matched the admiration that had poured from my mother's lips whenever she'd spoken of her mom.

Soon I learned that while my real grandmother was indeed kind, loving, and happy to welcome me to America, she was a *lot* shorter than the woman in the harbor.

God has called us to play a unique role here on earth. He's asked us to shower our friends and neighbors with stories about Him, testimonies of Him, and invitations from Him. He's depending on us to make Him so real to our hearers, so filled with love and kindness, that when they discover Him working in their lives or hear Him whispering in their ears, they'll recognize Him immediately.

That's why Jesus came to earth and lived among us, eating our food, wearing our clothes, sharing our sorrows. He wanted to show us, in no uncertain terms, what God is like.

What image of our heavenly Father do you share? What picture do your actions at home, at play, and in the workplace paint in people's minds? Will those who know you be able to recognize the God you worship based on your reflection of Him?

One Christian writer put it this way: "We cannot by searching find out God. But He has revealed Himself in the character of Christ, who is the brightness of the Father's glory and the express image of His person. If we desire a knowledge of God, we must be Christlike" (Ellen G. White, *Manuscript Releases,* vol. 21, p. 410).

The same is true if we desire to share Him with our world.

Success

Choose you this day whom ye will serve. Joshua 24:15.

I love to read autobiographies of famous people, especially those in media work. Musicians, actors, directors, writers, even presidents of large companies, fascinate me. But I've noticed something disturbing as I review their lives. In almost every case such men and women have had to make sacrifices on their way to success, sacrifices that could possibly cost them eternity.

An award-winning country singer insists in her autobiography that God is 100 percent in her life, yet the main theme of many of her best-selling hits is adultery, a subject God considers disgraceful. A much-respected and talented actor whom we've all seen on our television screens passionately proclaims that an all-loving God can't exist because the world is such a hate-filled place. His view of success doesn't include the very Being who made his life possible.

More often than not, high-level CEOs are working on their second or third marriages, having abandoned earlier families and home responsibilities in their push for power. Who has time for ball games, piano recitals, and romantic walks along the beach when one has to make a million dollars before the end of the fiscal year?

While their business and commercial acumen is excellent, their personal and spiritual lives suffer greatly. The God-created concepts of family and health become nothing more than nuisances, hindering their climb up the corporate ladder.

Even a biblical success story carries a familiar ring. Solomon, looking back on his life and accomplishments, writes, "Yet when I surveyed all that my hands had done and what I had toiled to achieve, everything was meaningless, a chasing after the wind; nothing was gained under the sun" (Ecclesiastes 2:11, NIV).

We've all got mortgages to pay, doctors to visit, food to buy. Each of us must succeed at some level in order to survive. But what, exactly, should we be willing to sacrifice along the way?

Booker T. Washington once said, "A measure of a man's success is not what he achieves, but what he overcomes." It sounds to me as if our country singer, popular actor, busy CEO, and even Solomon of old failed to realize that we must include, follow, and proclaim God and His laws in any grab for success. The unfortunate overachievers we have been looking at failed to overcome the deadly concept that God isn't important, that what He says doesn't matter, that we can live life on our own. They were all wrong.

Christian author Paul Rees writes, "If you want a picture of success as heaven measures it, don't look for the blaring of the bands on Broadway; listen, rather, for the tinkle of water splashing into a basin, while God incarnate, in a humility that makes angels hold their breath, sponges the grime from the feet of His undeserving disciples" *(Bible Expositor)*.

When Jesus comes back to earth, He won't invite us to heaven based on how well we've labored or how well we've lived. On that glorious day, our acceptance of salvation will hinge entirely on how well we've loved.

What's God's secret for success? To live lives focused on the sacrifices. All else is meaningless.

The Mother in "Our Father"

Now there stood by the cross of Jesus his mother. John 19:25.

The living room clock chimes twice, its solemn voice calling from what seems like a great distance. I lie very still, facing the window, staring out at the star-littered sky, trying to remember what it was like not to hurt, not to feel sick, not to be afraid.

My mother sleeps by my bed, her hand holding mine, her head resting against my knee. I listen to her slow, even breathing. She'd come in hours ago to stroke my fevered head. Her gentle touch always eased the uncertainty of sickness and made me believe that I would run and play again, that I'd feel hungry and want to do something other than hide beneath the covers. With the lullaby of her presence I close my eyes and fall asleep, secure in the knowledge that my mother will keep her silent vigil over me no matter how dark and long the night, no matter how painful the hurt.

Mother love. No count of miles, no passing of years, can outdistance the bond between a God-fearing mother and her child. As the world consumes itself with the darkness of hate, mother love remains the one clear light illuminating a multitude of lives.

We speak of God as "Our Father." But we can describe the Creator in more ways than that. Long ago He took a very special part of Himself and molded it into a being

17

called *mother*. Each mother's touch is His touch, each tear His tear.

A group of shepherds crowds around a wooden manger as a woman gently smooths the rough blanket placed about her newborn son. "Hush, little Jesus, don't cry," she whispers. "Your father and I are watching over You." The baby sleeps, comforted by the voice even in the presence of strangers.

Then we see another scene. The same mother stands at the foot of a Roman cross. High above, suspended by nails, the baby, now grown, hangs limp and lifeless. The woman doesn't move as she gazes at the still profile of her Son. Her lips form words long forgotten, a phrase too agonizing to utter aloud. "Hush, little Jesus," she whispers, "don't cry. Your Father and I are watching over You."

We're all children of God. In our world the imperfect love of Christian fathers and mothers represents a powerful echo of His affection for us. By their example we learn that we can feel safe and secure resting in the everlasting arms of our Creator. No matter how far we must travel, no matter how many oceans separate us from those we love, we can know that we've a heavenly Parent ready to sit by our side through the darkest night. When fear grips our hearts and our eyes fill with tears, that's the time to listen for the still small voice of Jesus saying to each one of us, "Hush, My child, don't cry. Your Father and I are watching over you."

Speeding Ticket

Moreover the law entered, that the offence might abound. But where sin abounded, grace did much more abound. Romans 5:20.

Traffic on the I-405 freeway wasn't heavy yet as I turned my motorcycle north and sprinted toward the Grapevine. I was leaving the smog-tainted atmosphere of Los Angeles for a weekend in Yosemite National Park, my favorite destination on earth.

As I passed Van Nuys, I noticed an all-too-familiar sight in my rearview mirror. Apparently one of Los Angeles County's finest thought my rate of escape from the San Fernando Valley was a little too eager, and wanted to spend some quality time with me.

"Where do you work?" the officer asked, making notations on his clipboard. I explained that I was a member of a film crew that produced Christ-centered television programs. His pen paused in midword. "I don't believe in religion," he said, finishing his scribbling and handing me a ticket. "How could God allow such suffering in the world?"

Feeling suddenly evangelistic, I responded, "What would you say if I told you that I wasn't going to pay this?" I held the paper up in front of him.

"Hey, you were speeding," he warned. "You gotta pay. That's the law."

"Then why should sinners who ignore God's protective laws, turn their backs on His warnings, even curse His name, get off free?" I asked. "We bring most suffering on our-selves. If we do the crime, we gotta do the time. I could've slowed down a little and not earned this ticket. All that was required was a relaxing of the wrist of my right hand. Should I now blame you because I have to cough up hard-earned money to pay for my error in judgment? Are you the bad guy here? Is this all your fault? Should I now hate you because I ended up with this invitation to support the county's law-enforcement efforts?"

My uniformed friend didn't answer. He just stood there by my motorcycle shaking his head slowly, letting the simple truth of God's law sink into his mind, allowing its timeless message to slip past years of excuses and anger, past the doubt and self-pity, past the ingrained traditional image of our heavenly Father. For the next hour we tarried by the center divider, the cop and the lawbreaker, discussing God and humanity, compar-ing our small encounter with the vast cosmic struggle going on between good and evil. The parallels were undeniable, the lessons to be learned real and tangible to us both.

The traffic patrol officer had become a god of sorts, defending the law against some-one who'd, for a moment, chosen to ignore it. I'd become the sinner, defiantly insisting that I knew best and could drive at any speed that fitted my desire to escape for the weekend. The ticket I held in my hand was a reminder that a law existed. To be totally honest about the matter, the whole system made perfect sense. Speed kills. Laws save lives, including mine.

Before we parted company, the police officer said he'd think about what we'd dis-cussed. Later, when I paid the ticket, so did I.

Service With a Smile

With good will doing service, as to the Lord, and not to men. Ephesians 6:7.

I remember how cool and damp the predawn air felt against my face as I walked past the big tent sitting ghostlike in the misty meadow. All the religious convocation attendees were still sleeping, save for the few, like me, who had early-morning duties to perform. Tables waited to be set, chairs to be arranged. The rising sun would summon hungry people to breakfast, where they'd fill their bodies with earthly nourishment before inviting preachers and teachers to feed their souls with spiritual food.

When they came, we were ready. My church school classmates and I would smile our welcome and offer to carry the trays of the elderly. Amid the warm banter filling the cafeteria, we'd mop up spills, bring fresh orange juice to the tables, find lost shawls, and tend the growling stainless-steel dishwasher, feeding it rack after rack of soiled silverware and oatmeal-encrusted bowls.

Three times a day we young people would gather in the kitchen to eat our own meals before the crowds arrived. That was our pay, along with an occasional trip into the big walk-in freezer with its cases of vegetables and inviting boxes of ice-cream sandwiches. Three times a day we'd fire up the machinery of food service. And three times a day we'd hand-dry hundreds of cups, saucers, plates, and spoons, and walk miles between the cashier and the tables, making sure everyone was happy and comfortable.

When I read Psalm 27:14, an Old Testament passage that invites us to "wait on the Lord: be of good courage, and he shall strengthen thine heart," I understand exactly what David meant when he said "wait." I know what it's like to *wait* on someone. It's a matter of doing everything you can to please that person. More milk? Be right back. Need another napkin? No problem. Sun too hot on you? Allow me to pull the shades down a bit. Here, let me carry that heavy tray for you. Are you sure you have enough toast?

Service with a smile. Eager to please. Making a person feel special even if they're a bit demanding. To me, that's what it means to wait.

As evening calm descended over the camp meeting grounds, I'd make my weary way back to the cabin that I shared with my older brothers, eager to spend some time with my latest purchase from the Christian bookstore. In the distance I could hear singing echoing through the trees, happy voices raised in praise to the God who made us all. As I listened I'd smile to myself. Those were my singers, my voices. I'd fed and cleaned up after them.

All the years that I worked at the cafeteria I continually found joy in knowing that my simple service to those dedicated men and women made their lives just a little bit better during their short camp meeting stay.

Waiting on people can be highly rewarding. And waiting on the Lord carries its own recompense as well. That particular joy will last throughout eternity.

The Crying Man

Comfort ye, comfort ye my people, saith your God. Isaiah 40:1.

Morning rush-hour drivers vied for position along the tangled maze of streets criss-crossing Silver Spring, Maryland. Already the temperature hovered around the 90-degree mark. It was going to be another hot, humid day in the city.

Tempers burned and horns blared as accountants, secretaries, bank presidents, and computer programmers inched toward downtown destinations, trying to ignore the brown haze that hung over the streets like an acid fog, taxing air-conditioners and lungs alike. So much work. So little time.

I took my place in the line of cars waiting to turn left onto Fenton Avenue, my mind running through a seemingly endless checklist of things to do that day. People depended on me as I waged budget battles and brought projects back on schedule.

That's when I saw him, a man in an expensive, three-piece suit standing on the corner, face buried in his hands. His broad shoulders sagged as his body swayed back and forth. Tousled brown hair flowed over his fingers as tiny drops of moisture squeezed through and fell silently to the sidewalk.

No one noticed. No one stopped. The crying man stood there alone in a sea of humanity.

He looked like a lost little boy. Glancing about, I half expected to see a kind-faced mother rush to his side and gather him up in her arms. The crying man would look into her comforting eyes and tell her of the pain ravaging his heart. But no one came. Cars eased past or idled impatiently by the curb, their drivers and passengers lost in sorrows of their own.

I stared at the scene for a long moment, moved by the passion of his distress. My arms ached to hold the man, to speak encouragement to him, to tell him that everything would be all right. But we were separated by traffic, by time, by tradition.

The sudden, angry blast of a horn drew my attention to the light as it changed from red to green. Pressing on the accelerator, I eased around the corner. In the rearview mirror I watched the crying man grow smaller and smaller. Then he was gone, swallowed up by the swirling mix of faces and vehicles, vanishing completely in the cold press of humanity and the terrible reality of modern life. I would never see him again. He would never know that I witnessed his tears, that I cared, that I loved him.

"Oh, Lord," I prayed through tears of my own, "comfort the crying man. Forgive my life so filled with deadlines and responsibilities. Forgive me for letting the expectations of others keep me from acting on Your impulse. Bring me another crying man. Please. Give me another chance."

Again I looked around at the faces rushing by. But this time I was searching.

Get Up!

Therefore thou shalt hear the word at my mouth,
and warn them from me. Ezekiel 33:7.

One day a pilot in training at an Austrian aviation school took off on a practice flight. For an hour or so he steered his little airplane through a series of climbs, turns, stalls, and other procedures assigned by the instructor who'd sent him skyward. The student was feeling pretty good about the flight as he worked to hone his skills and improve his coordination. The air felt smooth. His craft responded without hesitation to his control.

All was going well until he slipped a bit too low over a section of the countryside while executing a particularly difficult maneuver. With a sickening twang, his canvas-covered craft sliced through some high-tension wires bordering a lake. In an instant he and his machine plunged into the waves and flipped over. What had started out as a routine training mission had become a life-and-death struggle in the blink of an eye.

Miraculously, the inexperienced pilot managed to free himself from the sinking airplane and struggle to shore. While sitting on the rocks trying to regain his senses, the hapless aviator noticed that the wires through which his airplane had sliced now lay snapping and sparking across a shiny line of railroad tracks. That's when he heard the distant whistle of the Vienna Express. The stage was set for yet another disaster.

Even though in pain and suffering from multiple injuries, the pilot rose and stumbled down the tracks, madly waving his leather hat. The conductor saw the signal and the train skidded to a halt just in time, saving many lives.

Ever felt like that pilot? You're sitting on some emotional rocks bruised and bleeding, having just escaped an unfortunate predicament, trying to figure out how in the world you got yourself into such a mess, when you notice yet another danger lurking nearby. Suddenly you hear the sound of an approaching train.

"They deserve what they get," you're tempted to say. "I mean, look at me. I'm in terrible shape. I've been treated unfairly. Nobody cares. The whole world is out to get me!"

Then you remember a long-forgotten image of a Saviour hanging on a tree, His body twisted in pain, life forces slowly ebbing away. He turns and looks at you. "Forgive him, Father," you hear Him say. "Forgive him."

No matter how wounded we are, no matter what evil has done to us, no matter how much we've managed to mess up our lives, God needs us. There's still a place for us in His ongoing mission of salvation. Express trains filled with unsuspecting passengers race toward oblivion. Souls teeter on the edge of eternity. Wires sprawl across the tracks.

"Wave your hat," God calls to each one of us. "No matter how you feel, I still love you. No matter what you've done or how much you've managed to injure yourself, Satan is setting traps. Get up. *Get up!* There's a world to warn!"

True Value

Every good gift and every perfect gift is from above,
and cometh down from the Father of lights. James 1:17.

It was the most wonderful train set my 10-year-old eyes had ever seen: big black engine puffing real smoke, loud whistle announcing its passage through the little station complete with passengers holding tiny suitcases, coal cars following in neat order, each swaying from side to side as they maneuvered around the curve.

A well-dressed man standing beside me studied the display for a long moment and then sauntered over to the salesman. "I'll take it," I heard him say as he reached for his wallet.

"Well, of course you'll take it," I breathed. "It's the most perfect gift any dad could give a kid for Christmas."

Before the evening was over, I made sure my father visited the toy store three times. Perhaps he'd catch the Lionel bug if exposed to it enough. I wanted that train set as much as I'd ever wanted anything! All my dad had to do was walk over to the salesman and say those magic words.

The next few weeks were pure agony. But at long last Christmas morning arrived. My parents ordered me to stay in my room while they "finished decorating the tree,"

27

an action that confirmed my hope that something special would be waiting. Finally I descended the stairs. What I saw made me squeal with glee. There, circling the cloth-covered base of our brightly lit evergreen, rumbling around on shiny silver tracks, was a steam engine pulling a line of boxcars.

"Yes!" I shouted, racing across the room and dropping to my knees at the tree. "Oh yes, oh yes, oh *yes!*"

However, my joy quickly turned to concern. On closer inspection I noticed that the engine wasn't as magnificent as I remembered. The wheels weren't as detailed, the cars not as real-looking. Where was the smoke and the whistle? This wasn't my train. It wasn't a Lionel!

"Do you like it?" Dad asked, kneeling beside me and watching the coal cars slip past. "I wanted to buy the one you showed me at the toy store, but it cost far more than we could afford. With your brothers in college and you and Susie in church school, we just don't have any extra money." He pointed encouragingly. "See, it came with a couple plastic logs for the flatcar. Neat, huh?"

My dream had shattered. Instead of the mighty Lionel, I'd been presented with a substitute, a fake, an also-ran. But a little voice seemed to be speaking to me from somewhere deep in my disappointment. It reminded me that 10-year-old boys must sometimes accept what's real even when dreams are more exciting. Perhaps a kid like me needed to learn that a father's sacrifice is more valuable than a son's desire.

I watched the little train rumble around the base of the tree, then turned and looked into the eyes of the man who'd given me the best he could afford. "Dad," I said, "it's the most wonderful train set in the world."

Memories of the Journey

To them who by patient continuance in well-doing seek for glory and honour and immortality, [is rendered] eternal life. Romans 2:7.

My wife and her family were planning an extended trip through Ohio, Indiana, and Michigan to visit old haunts and renew family ties. Dorinda's niece and nephew, Megan (7) and Zachary (4), were asked by their mother if they wanted to come along.

"It's so far," the youngsters moaned in chorus. "We'll be riding in the car forever!"

"But Aunt Dorinda will be in Ohio waiting for you," their mother said.

Two sets of eyes opened wide. "Aunt Dorinda? Really?" they gasped. "We're going!"

What happened to the long car ride? What happened to the cramped quarters and dirty roadside restrooms? What happened to the motion sickness and truck fumes? All that didn't matter anymore. Aunt Dorinda would be waiting in a place called "Ohio." The expected reunion drove the two children to a quick and enthusiastic decision in favor of the trip.

Strange how anticipation of what's waiting at the end can ease a journey.

My oldest brother and I once jumped into his minivan in Sacramento, California, and headed east over the mountains. He was returning to his family after a long business trip, and I was headed for the altar. I knew Dorinda was eagerly waiting for me as she busied herself finalizing wedding plans and confirming arrangements for our honeymoon cottage in the Great Smoky Mountains. In my mind's eye I could see her enjoying bridal showers and other special events organized in her honor. She and her mom were making the rounds of local shopping malls and little out-of-the-way stores searching for just the right decorations and other particulars designed to make the approaching day memorable for everyone involved.

The miles my brother and I traveled may have seemed endless to someone else. We simply ignored them. We regarded those barren stretches of Nevada and Utah only as necessary evils. The flatlands of Nebraska and Iowa slipped unconcerned beneath our tires as we traveled day and night on our way to Chicago, where I'd catch my flight to Tennessee.

At long last, when I wrapped my young bride-to-be in my arms, the roads and bumps and fast food were but a fading memory. I had reached my goal. The journey was over. My heart felt only happiness.

Something tells me that when we find ourselves enveloped in the arms of Jesus, we'll not count the miles we traveled. The heartache, pain, doubts, and fears will vanish from our thoughts in an instant. When we as God's children brush the dust of generations of sin from our shoes and stand redeemed before His throne, joy and relief will so fill our minds that there won't be any room for self-pity. Memories of the journey will fade away, eclipsed completely by glorious anticipation of the eternal destination ahead.

Just in Case

Beloved, if God so loved us, we ought also to love one another. 1 John 4:11.

Why are you doing this?" I asked my aging father one bright, crisp autumn day. "You've got a perfectly good furnace. Surely you can afford heating oil."

"Yes," he stated as he took aim at a log teetering atop a stump and then sliced his ax through the dry wood with a resounding crack, "but one of you kids might need help down the road."

"We're doing fine," I protested. "We've all got jobs and are paying the bills. Why don't you and Mom take it easy? Spend your money on fun things. Live a little."

"Wood's cheaper 'n oil," my father continued, ignoring my plea. "It's nice to have a little set aside for you guys just in case."

Just in case? My father was splitting wood he didn't have to cut and working hard to save money he didn't have to just so he could help children who didn't need any assistance. But that's the way it had always been. Growing up, I'd seen my dad face some pretty rough times, insisting that my three siblings and I attend Christian schools when public education would have been much cheaper. I'd watched him work long hours to earn the simple salary of a pastor, spending evenings and weekends in service to the God he loved. Countless nights I'd hear the garage door open as I stirred from slumber, signaling that my dad had finally returned home after yet another endless day at the conference office.

Unusual? Yes. Unique? Not to God. My heavenly Father understands such strange behavior. He figured there'd be those who might need Him, so He allowed His Son to leave heaven—just in case.

Jesus was born as a babe, just in case a child cried out in the night needing comfort. Our Saviour grew up under the watchcare of human parents, just in case a lonely boy or girl needed a father's love. He walked among the poor and sick just in case a hurting heart longed to feel His healing touch. The Redeemer studied the religious teachings of the world just in case a pastor or priest needed answers to heart-troubling questions. And Jesus slept in the elements, just in case a downcast voice moaned from a park bench or cold hard sidewalk.

Our Saviour allowed Himself to be sold for 30 pieces of silver, just in case a soul in slavery yearned to be free. He felt the sharp pain of the whip, just in case a whimper arose from a prison cell. The Master stood unspeaking before lying witnesses, just in case a child of God was accused unjustly. And in that terrible hour, the Creator of the universe died the agonizing death of a sinner, just in case there was a soul to save.

I watched my father chopping wood and suddenly felt the power of that love on reserve for me in heaven, just in case I needed it.

Heavenly Music

Wherefore shew ye to them, and before the churches,
the proof of your love. 2 Corinthians 8:24.

An eerie mixture of sounds echoed across the college campus as I ran toward the old wooden music building. Inside students puffed on shiny trumpets, pounded on deep-throated drums, and vibrated reeds attached firmly to mouthpieces as each tried to prepare for the workout to come.

"We're going to look at a new piece today," the conductor announced as I tried to slip unseen to my chair, carrying the long, tubelike bassoon, that year's instrument of choice. It wasn't that I was a great player. Hardly. The band simply needed the nasal tones of a bassoon, and I accepted the challenge.

Jack McClarty smiled down from his perch on the little platform fronting the rehearsal hall. His enthusiasm was contagious. Every member of the band respected his talent and enjoyed his energetic conducting.

As I opened the sheet music that had been placed on my stand, I expected to find my usual collection of supporting notes and passages designed for the bassoon. But one glance stopped my heart midbeat. There, right above the first passages of the piece, I saw: "Duet—Bassoon and Piccolo."

Duet? Me? And *my* bassoon? I glanced over at the piccolo player, a woman who happened to be a great musician. She was also the conductor's wife.

"Let's give it a quick run-through," Jack McClarty called out, lifting his long baton—a signal for everyone to hoist whatever instrument they possessed to their lips. Obediently I positioned the bassoon's double reeds above my tongue, tried to make sense of the notes dancing across the page, and placed my fingers over the holes that I hoped would produce those notes. When the baton fell, the piccolo player and I launched into our duet.

Mice ran from the building.

The conductor's wife did great. One could best describe my contribution as "interesting."

"Sounds like you need to spend some quality time with this one," the band director whispered to me at the close of practice. "You'll do great. You'll see."

Since I was a communications major, my world revolved around cameras, video equipment, the college radio station, and the favorite pastime of all members of the male student population—girls. Who had time to practice? The choice was simple. Either I give up something or continue to make a complete fool of myself in front of the other members of the band.

So I cut way down on the communications stuff and began seeking out deserted rooms located far from human ears. There I practiced and practiced, cheeks puffing, lips spitting, fingers fumbling over the shiny metal levers running the length of the bassoon. I squeaked and squawked, fluttered and buzzed, chortled and warbled the notes of the duet again and again until my face hurt.

I did improve, beginning to hit more notes than I missed. But I was far from perfect. During practice sessions with the band I'd look over at the piccolo player and hope she wasn't totally embarrassed by being linked musically to me for the first portion of the piece. Amazingly, she didn't seem to mind as she weaved back and forth, adding her lilting, melodious notes to my ponderous renditions.

Then it happened. Jack McClarty passed out the programs for our upcoming concert at Forest Lake Academy in Florida. There, launching us into the second half of our presentation, was "the piece." I couldn't believe my eyes. He actually wanted me to play a duet with his wife in a live concert. In front of people!

"You'll do fine," he said, responding to my protest.

"I'll bomb and take us all with me," I countered.

"Just play like you enjoy it," he insisted.

The big night approached. We traveled from what was then Southern Missionary College to the tree-lined campus of Forest Lake Academy. Even as I enjoyed the warm sunshine and friendly people at the school, my mind was elsewhere, playing endlessly that dumb duet. How could the conductor do this to me? Forget that. How could he do it to his wife?

We played that night to a packed house. Serving as the band announcer, I introduced the numbers, reading from a carefully prepared script, informing our listeners of when the next number was written, by whom, and for whom. And then . . .

McClarty stepped proudly onto his little platform as each of us lifted our instruments to our lips. The band was ready. But the first 15 seconds of the piece belonged to the bassoon and piccolo. At the downbeat we began our duet.

I don't know what McClarty heard. It couldn't possibly have been me. But at the end of our passage, he glanced in my direction and gave me a quick thumbs-up as a broad smile wrinkled his face. Hadn't he noticed the squeak? Hadn't he heard that very obvious chortle? He must've cringed when I played that third note as a sharp when it was supposed to be a flat. However, from his reaction, I'd just sailed through that duet like a pro, adding beauty to his program.

That night was a long time ago. Decades have passed since I've held a bassoon in my hands. But the memories came back to me in a rush the day I heard that Jack McClarty had died of a heart attack. Time is a great teacher, and I now realize something my favorite conductor taught me without saying a word. When I played that duet with trembling fingers before our expectant audience, he wasn't listening to the notes. He was listening to the hard work and the practice I'd put into the piece. McClarty was hearing what no one else could hear. On that warm Florida night he listened lovingly to the notes of a student who was doing the best he could. To Jack McClarty that was beautiful music.

Someday in heaven I plan to thank my friend again for his acceptance of my faults and for being a living, breathing echo of my heavenly Conductor. If he decides to put together a band, I'll be there, ready to add my grateful notes to his praise.

Forgiving Love

For if ye forgive men their trespasses,
your heavenly Father will also forgive you. Matthew 6:14.

I didn't catch her name, but her image will remain with me for a long, long time. The news report flickering across the television screen showed her sitting in a hospital bed, wrapped in bandages, smiling bravely.

Earlier that day the young girl had come across a stray bear cub sitting forlornly in a tree. She'd tried to help it down. That's when the cub had bitten her.

Understandably, the doctors were worried. Did the animal have rabies? Only one way existed to find out. Kill the cub and do some tests.

"No!" the little girl protested.

"That means we'll have to give you rabies treatments," the medical experts responded. "They hurt pretty bad."

"I don't care," the child insisted. "Just don't kill the cub. He didn't know what he was doing."

Here was a little girl from New Mexico who was willing to endure needless pain and suffering in order to save the life of the bear cub that had bitten her.

Where did she learn that? Who planted such an unreasonable response in her mind? Certainly not the world with its glorification of revenge. "An eye for an eye, and a tooth for a tooth!" generations have shouted as they picked up stones, swords, and heat-seeking missiles to hurl at their latest enemy. The soil carpeting every continent has absorbed the blood of countless people.

Somewhere within the present city of Jerusalem rests a tiny plot of earth that long ago accepted the blood of a dying Man who'd been brutalized by the wild nature of humanity. In His ears echoed the hateful taunts and evil laughter of those He'd come to redeem. But as He drew His final breath, He gasped, "Father, forgive them, for they don't know what they're doing."

Forgiving love. No greater power exists in the entire universe. No splitting of the atom, no burst of supernova energy, can compete with the simple act of forgiveness. Lives change, long-cherished animosities vanish, hearts once burdened with guilt and shame begin to beat anew. You can see the transformation on the faces of children as they look to you for acceptance after they've strayed from your commands. "Do you still love me?" they wordlessly ask. "Am I still your little boy or little girl? Will things ever be the same again?" Forgiveness answers those questions with a resounding *yes*.

A husband sits face in hands after an ugly confrontation with his wife. Hurtful words have flown, unmerited accusations have been hurled, promises have been broken. Then he feels her gentle touch on his shoulder, and the tears flow. Her simple words "I forgive you" open the floodgates of hope and healing.

Somewhere in New Mexico a young bear grew up in the wild, free to live its life as nature dictates. And in my tiny corner of the world I'm free to live my life because Someone was willing to endure undeserved pain for me. You and I exist because we've been forgiven.

Our Laughing God

To every thing there is a season . . .
a time to weep, and a time to laugh. Ecclesiastes 3:1-4.

It probably happens every day. Those nearest to the throne in heaven hear the unmistakable and joyous sound of the God of the universe laughing. I imagine it's a wondrous sound, filled with deep love and pure delight.

Why is He laughing? Because of us. We do some really funny things.

Take church bulletins, for instance. Sometimes we print lines that don't quite work on paper. Imagine the surprise when one group of saints read, "Don't let worry kill you. Let the church help." Or try to picture the snickers when this announcement appeared: "This afternoon there will be a meeting in the south and north ends of the church. Children will be baptized at both ends."

How about this springtime literary gem: "This being Easter Sunday, we will ask Mrs. Lewis to come forward and lay an egg on the altar."

It must have been hard for the choir to sing the Sabbath their church bulletin contained the following insert: "Eight new choir robes are currently needed, due to the addition of several new members and to the deterioration of some older ones."

And who will ever forget the day the congregation read, "For those who have children and don't know it, we have a nursery downstairs"?

I wish I could have seen the reaction to this printed announcement: "At the evening service tonight, the topic will be 'What Is Hell?' Come early and listen to the choir practice." The soloist must have been one of those deteriorating members mentioned earlier.

Giving may have been particularly brisk after the following proclamation appeared: "Next Sunday a special collection will be taken to defray the cost of the new carpet. All those wishing to do something on the carpet will come forward and do so."

No group seems to be immune. One forward-thinking assembly of believers announced in their bulletin: "The eighth graders will be presenting Shakespeare's *Hamlet* in the basement on Friday at 7:00 p.m. The congregation is invited to attend this tragedy."

One week this jewel appeared in glorious black and white: "The Reverend Adams spoke briefly, much to the delight of his audience." Could he have been the same pastor who was the subject of another slip of the computer key? "The preacher will preach his farewell message, after which the choir will sing, 'Break Forth With Joy.'" Or perhaps he had to endure this printed insert: "During the absence of our pastor, we enjoyed the rare privilege of hearing a good sermon when A. B. Doe supplied our pulpit." I believe that the carefully crafted mood of one particular service may have shattered when it was declared to all that "the service will close with 'Little Drops of Water.' One of the ladies will start quietly and the rest of the congregation will join in."

Perhaps this person was part of the group belonging to this announcement: "The ladies of the church have cast off clothing of every kind. They can be seen in the church basement."

Does God laugh? I'm sure He does, in innocent and loving fun. I can see Him walking the golden streets, shaking His beautiful head from side to side, a wide grin spread across His face as He recounts something one of us did or said. Such moments only deepen His love for us and strengthen His resolve to bring us home to live with Him forever.

Besides, where do you think *we* learned such a strange skill? Our laughter can and should be a continuous and life-healing echo of God's love.

Blind Faith

*And in that day shall the deaf hear the words of the book, and the eyes
of the blind shall see out of obscurity, and out of darkness. Isaiah 29:18.*

Picture a summer camp filled with motorboats, canoes, horses, archery ranges, and nature trails. Then imagine that camp filled with young people—all happy, all energetic, all blind.

Christian Record International, a nonprofit organization based in Lincoln, Nebraska,
operates over two dozen such camps in the United States and Canada each year. On-site
preparations begin long before the campers arrive. The staffs fill in holes and remove tree
stumps. Workers string ropes between cabins and the main buildings, providing a tactile
highway for the children.

When the big day arrives, the young people come by the busload, each boy and girl
breathlessly eager to sample the adventures waiting for them. "How tall are you? Can
we go swimming? Will you teach me how to water-ski? What's a horse look like?" Such
questions saturate the first few hours of their stay.

Perhaps the one activity sighted people think is impossible for a blind person to master is water-skiing. Many of the children have never swum in a lake, much less skimmed

over one at 20 miles an hour while balancing on two long boards attached to their feet. But these campers don't believe in impossible. I've seen beaming boys and girls rising on wobbly legs as an instructor skies alongside shouting encouragement. Most get and stay up on their first or second try!

Archery? Balloons tied to targets reward good aim with a loud *pop*.

Kickball? No problem when using a special ball with a built-in beeper.

Nature trails? Touches, tastes, smells, and sounds make hikes memorable.

Who needs to see a bonfire to enjoy its warmth? Or who needs eyes to experience the glory of a stack of hotcakes smothered in maple syrup? One camper told a friend that "this place must be beautiful because it smells so nice." I heard another playfully lament that he was a born loser. When asked why, he stated, "I'm blind and I'm scared of the dark."

But nothing compares with talent night. On this particular evening joy knows no bounds. The master of ceremonies calls out a name, and the whole camp erupts into wild cheering. Someone leads a child to the microphone, at which he or she announces, "Tonight I'm going to tell a joke," or "Tonight I'm going to sing." My personal favorite was the little boy who told his audience, "Right now I'm going to make a funny face." He did. The gathering roared with laughter.

Did these special children need to see a camp to enjoy it? No. Then do we need to see God to enjoy Him, to revel in His presence, to feel comfortable in His care? Not if we allow our hearts and our minds to recognize His power even though we can't yet gaze upon Him with our eyes.

We can sense His comfort and listen to His words echoing from the lips of friends or the pages of the Bible. And we can know that He's with us because He's promised never to leave us. Blind faith doesn't need to see. It simply believes.

No Way Out

Part 1

*There is a way which seemeth right unto a man,
but the end thereof are the ways of death. Proverbs 14:12.*

MOTORIST GRABBED BY ATLANTIC OCEAN
BOY DOOMED TO DIE UNLESS HE DRINKS GALLON OF WATER
X-RAY TECH ATTACKED BY OWN MACHINE
CHRISTIAN CONTEMPLATES SUICIDE

Sensational headlines? Tabloid trash screaming at you from the checkout counter? The lead stories for the evening edition of late-breaking news? Maybe. But the first three headlines are true.

As Alice Hall, of Bar Harbor, Maine, drove home from work she decided to take a shortcut along the shore. One problem, though. Alice had forgotten just how fast tides can rush in. Crossing a spit of sand, she suddenly found herself hubcap-deep in salt water. *I'll just speed through it,* the woman thought to herself.

But the ocean proved faster than her car. In minutes waves pounded against her

42

door panels. Her wheels lost traction, and she was stuck.

Young Walter Koester felt his feet slip. He looked up just in time to see tons of earth falling straight at him. In seconds he had been buried up to his waist, with more dirt and rocks on the way.

Walter's father, who was working nearby, snatched the only thing he could find—a garden hose—and threw it into the rapidly filling pit. Just as his son grabbed the loose end dangling by his head, the landslide completely buried the boy under eight feet of earth.

In the darkness Walter jammed the end of the hose into his mouth and tried to take a breath. Unfortunately, the garden hose was full of water. He was in big trouble.

Frank Brown, an X-ray technician working at Bellevue Hospital in New York City, instructed his patient to lie still on the table. The female nurse in attendance, Grace Fusco, watched Frank switch off the machine so he could make some minor adjustments. But the electrical system had a short somewhere.

X-ray expert Brown suddenly found his hand closing a circuit, and 75,000 volts of electricity coursed through him like a deadly river. In an instant he couldn't speak or move. The man collapsed, his hand held tightly by the angry power surging through the cables.

Ashen-faced, the patient leaped to the floor and rushed from the room. The nurse, acting on impulse, ran to the technician and grabbed his shoulders. The same 75,000 volts hit her like a speeding bus, knocking her backward across the room and against the wall.

Twice Grace tried to rescue the man held in the fiery grip of the current. And twice she felt herself slammed against the far wall. She was about to lose consciousness, and Frank Brown was about to die.

You've had all you can stand. Life's just too much to bear. Everything—*everything*—seems designed to hurt you, to destroy you, to keep you from finding any happiness at all.

Your coworkers laugh and seem to be enjoying life. Friends act unconcerned. The preacher at church never says anything you need to hear.

All is lost. If something doesn't happen soon, you'll end your own life. That's the only answer to this hopeless situation.

Right?

No Way Out

Part 2

In my distress I cried unto the Lord, and he heard me. Psalm 120:1.

As the water continued to rise, Alice Hall looked desperately around the confines of her slowly sinking car. She had no flashlight, no CB, no cellular phone or any other way of communicating with the shore.

Her hand bumped the steering wheel, causing the horn to toot. Wait. The horn. But people on the dark shore would just think someone was calling a friend or telling another driver to get out of the way. Unless . . .

Captain Fred Hayes, a mariner living by the ocean, tilted his head to one side and flipped off his radio. What was he hearing? Suddenly he paled. The horn in the distance was blaring out a code, the international distress signal known to all seafarers. *TOOT-TOOT-TOOT, T-O-O-T, T-O-O-T, T-O-O-T, TOOT-TOOT-TOOT.*

Rushing from his house, he spotted the car in the breakers. Quickly he called some friends, located a boat, and hurried to the rescue. Alice continued sending the signal until she saw the approaching skiff.

The rescuers saved the woman just as the tide completely enveloped her car with watery arms.

Walter Koester knew that if he wanted to breathe fresh air from above, he was going to have to drink the water in the garden hose. So he swallowed as fast as he could, forcing into his stomach at least a gallon of liquid.

After the hose had drained dry, he could breathe a little at a time. Soon rescuers attached a portable oxygen tank to the other end. After two long agonizing hours, Walter was free, shaken, and not at all thirsty.

The commotion in the X-ray room suggested to another technician that something was wrong next door. Rushing down the hallway, he burst into the chamber. What he saw horrified him. Then he did a highly scientific thing—not as heroic as the wild courage of the nurse, but much more effective. He jumped to the master switch on the wall and shut off all electricity to the room.

Frank Brown slumped totally unconscious onto the floor. Although he was suffering from burns and shock, he would recover. The nurse escaped with only bruises.

You think about your own situation. Who'll hear your SOS ringing out over the rising waves? Who's going to throw a garden hose in your direction as the earth falls and the lights go out? Who's going to rush in and switch off the powers that seem determined to destroy your life?

There's no way out. You're helpless, hopeless, lost.

Wait. You see a Man running toward you, hands outstretched. "At last," you shout. "Here comes my Rescuer."

But then the Man gets caught by an angry mob and nailed to a cross. You look up at Him, and He gazes down at you. "I'm here," He whispers. "I'm here to save you."

Sometimes, when all else fails, you have to trust the Man who once learned for Himself that there's always a way out.

Rock of Ages

For thou art my rock and my fortress;
therefore for thy name's sake lead me, and guide me. Psalm 31:3.

They weren't supposed to be on the mountain. Because of the danger and loss of life associated with this particular area of the Alps, the Swiss authorities had proclaimed the Wall of the Ogre off-limits to all climbers. But four youths, two Austrian and two German, had slipped past the barriers and were now clinging to the sheer cliff thousands of feet above astonished onlookers.

Suddenly the four excitement-seekers vanished from view as a cloud descended over the mountain. Within moments four lives found themselves in desperate peril, for that cloud, so innocent at first, proved to be the leading edge of a blizzard.

For two and a half days the Wall of the Ogre remained locked in a terrific battle with the elements. Winds screamed, icy rain and heavy snows blasted against the stones, and temperatures plummeted. The four climbers clung to the vertical face of the cliff, jamming themselves onto a tiny rock shelf carved by time and weather. No one could hear their shouts nor could anyone reach them. They remained hidden by the storm.

At long last the winds died down, and the heavy mists began to lift. Near exhaustion and suffering from exposure, the four young adventurers inched their way higher and higher, carving foot and handholds into the cliff with their ice axes. They eventually reached the top, lucky to be alive and ending in triumph the most spectacular mountaineering exploit of their lives.

When Old Testament David wrote many of his heart-rending poems, he was hiding in a cave somewhere, trying to live another day. King Saul and his army were searching the hills and valleys for the young man, ready to plunge their knives and spears into his chest. Saul harbored great jealousy toward the shepherd-turned-warrior. Hating him, he wanted to rid his kingdom of David's vibrant and handsome smile.

David understood what it was like to cling to stone as danger swirled about him. He often found shelter in its shadow and safety deep within it. So when he labeled God as a rock, he was lovingly applying those same attributes to his heavenly Father. "You are my rock," he wrote again and again. "In Your arms I find comfort and peace."

Clinging to a rock or hiding in a cave didn't stop evil from relentlessly pursuing Israel's future king. Neither does hiding ourselves in Jesus bring bad things to an end today. Winds still blow, fires still burn, tears still flow. But even in endless tumult we have a Foundation on which to stand, a Solid Rock on which to secure our lives. We find peace only as we press ourselves into the cleft of God's care and wait out the storms while securely resting in His mighty arms.

Reluctant Heroes

Thou shalt call his name JESUS:
for he shall save his people from their sins. Matthew 1:21.

Miners Harry Reid and Carl Myers lit the fuse and then ran. They'd just completed placing a series of 11 dynamite charges in an 85-foot mineshaft. It was definitely time to be somewhere else. But before Harry could make it to safety, the first charge went off prematurely, hurling him unconscious through flying splinters and tumbling rock. Carl spun around and shouted for his friend, but received no response. Then he saw his companion slumped against the cave wall.

Running back through the choking dust, Carl picked up his benumbed coworker, tossed him across his shoulder, and started up the steep 25-foot slope leading to safety. It was a muscle-straining effort. Just as Carl and his human cargo reached the mouth of the mine, the rest of the dynamite roared.

When the mine owners announced that they were going to recommend Carl Myers for the Carnegie Award of Heroism, the man just growled, "Keep the medal. Harry's alive, isn't he?"

A killer fire raced through a Brooklyn, New York, apartment house. A passing automobile skidded to a stop and a man jumped out, dashed into the burning building, and dragged, one after another, six people to safety.

When it was all over, a policeman asked for his name. "Never mind that," the reluctant hero replied impatiently as he headed for his car. "I'm late for work. Gotta go."

With that he sped away down the street.

Fourteen-year-old Boy Scout Allan Taylor and his dad were sound asleep in a hotel on Long Island, New York, when the boy awoke with a suspicious odor tickling his nostrils. Hopping out of bed, he peeked into the hallway and saw that it was filled with smoke. At that moment words he'd read in his Scout manual surfaced in his mind.

Without hesitating, he got two handkerchiefs, wet them under the faucet, gave one to his dad, tied the other over his nose and mouth, then ran down the corridors of the hotel tapping on the doors and saying calmly, "Better get dressed and get out. There's a little fire. Nothing to be excited about. Nothing serious."

After awakening everyone, he ran to the lobby and joined his father, where everybody organized a bucket brigade. His actions averted a panic and saved many people from suffocation. His response to their gratitude? "Please don't try to make a hero out of me. What I did was just routine Scout stuff."

Long ago Jesus Christ hung on a Roman cross in an all-out effort to save humanity. He suffered greatly and finally closed His eyes in death. Two days later, after walking triumphantly from His garden tomb, He met a weeping woman overcome with grief.

"Why are you crying?" He asked.

With tears clouding her vision, the visitor thought the speaker was the gardener. "They've stolen my Jesus," she sobbed. "Do you know where they've laid Him?"

Christ smiled and spoke her name softly. "Mary." The woman immediately recognized the Saviour and fell at His feet.

"Tell the others that I'm going home to see our Father," He whispered.

Jesus didn't ask for accolades. He didn't request a medal or covet a certificate of merit. Two days after His greatest act of bravery and courage, His only thoughts were to bring comfort to others and see His heavenly Father. Reluctant heroes never crave the spotlight. Success is reward enough.

The New Coat

Greater love hath no man than this,
that a man lay down his life for his friends. John 15:13.

A sizzling summer sun hangs over the small North Carolina town. Afternoon shoppers seek the cool recesses of air-conditioned stores and eateries. No dog barks, no bird flies as sidewalks and streets reflect the sun's rays in shimmering waves, making the surface of the town seem almost waterlike.

I sit just inside the front door of a small store wishing for a breeze—any breeze. Above the entrance hangs a sign. "Community Services Center." Business is slow. It's been an hour since anyone ventured in to browse through the "pre-owned" clothes hanging in neat rows throughout the small establishment.

My mind struggles in the heat, trying to remember the moment when I'd agreed to watch the store. "Community service? No problem," I'd said. "I'll be happy to keep an eye on things next Tuesday. Can't do enough for our poor and needy. Why, it's my Christian duty."

Nobody had said it was going to be so hot!

The presence of someone standing in front of me brings my thoughts back to the present.

51

"You open for business, young man?" His words seem more a reminder than a question.

"Yes, sir!" I announce, untangling myself from the chair and jumping to my feet. "What can I do for you?"

The man walks toward the first row of colorful clothes waiting on the rack. "I need a new coat."

"You're in luck," I say, guiding him to the rear of the store. "We have a great selection. Not much call for coats just now. You can have the whole rack to yourself. Take your time."

I watch him slowly sort through the garments, carefully scrutinizing each selection. His rough, work-worn hands appraise each seam and stitch, mentally comparing the handiwork against his personal checklist of requirements for a new coat.

The caked mud and clay clinging to his torn shoes and the deep weathered lines in his face reveal that he's a field worker, rotating from farm to farm, picking, planting, harvesting, bending in the hot sun day after endless day. Probably he'd done such backbreaking work since childhood.

"Have anything in blue? My wife likes blue."

His question takes me by surprise. For some reason I'd always assumed that poor people didn't care what color clothes they wore.

"I think I saw a blue one this morning," I say, looking at the man. "Let me help you find it." I start to sort through the garments. Suddenly for the first time I really see the coats on the rack. The colors are faded on many of them, the threads worn. I become uneasy as I realize that the man wants a coat he can wear so his wife will think he's handsome and say so. The garment will be his label to the world, his statement to society.

The man has crossed the room and is picking through the items on the bargain table. I study him for a long moment.

From deep within me anger begins to rise. Why does this man have to be poor? Why does anyone have to depend on the labels of others to form their own identity? That bargain table contains things that no one wants—a chipped teacup, a battered picture frame, an umbrella that won't stay open. Why must he depend on rejected treasures to add meaning to his world?

"Did you find one? My wife will be so pleased." He looks at me expectantly.

"See what you think of this," I say, holding out the best blue coat I can find.

The man slips his arms into the garment and adjusts the lapel. Turning to the left, and then to the right, he eyes himself in the broken mirror hanging on the wall.

"This is pretty nice," he says with genuine excitement. "Whatta ya think? Does it fit OK?" He turns toward me with an unbelievable look of satisfaction on his face.

My mind can't form an answer. I open my mouth, but words refuse to come out. The coat is old and worn. Some well-meaning, churchgoing, hymn-singing man wore the life out of that garment and then with great humility offered it to those who must live without.

"It seems to be the right size, doesn't it?" the man continues, glancing at the mirror again. "My wife can make adjustments if she has the right color thread."

I turn away as unwelcome tears sting my eyes. In my pocket rattles enough loose change to buy him three of those old coats. He's worked hard and come to me to buy a garment that I wouldn't be seen in.

"How much?" he asks. "I think it's just what I've been looking for."

"The price is written on that tag attached to the sleeve," I say, trying to control my feelings.

"Oh yes, let's see, says $1. Yeah, I've got that much." The man reaches into the pocket of his soiled and tattered trousers and draws out assorted nickels, dimes, and pennies. He places his wealth on the table and starts to count.

I want to scream, "Mister, take all the clothes you want! Take the red coats and the black coats. Take pants and shirts, too. They're all free today, no charge. Please, mister, don't be poor anymore. Stop depending on what other people reject to dress yourself, to furnish your house, to label your life. It shouldn't take all you have just to buy an old coat that someone else has worn out. Use your money to get your wife something nice, something special. It's not fair—it's just not fair!"

"Ninety-eight, ninety-nine, one dollar, just enough. Oh, this is wonderful. I've needed a new coat since last fall. Here you are, young man, $1. Thanks." I take his money and watch him walk to the front of the store. At the door he turns. "I'll be back next summer," he says. "Thanks again for your help."

In that moment a new and wonderful truth begins to light the dark question of my mind. An old coat is a new coat when you've spent everything you have to make it yours. "Mister," I say, "your blue coat—it's very nice. Looks good on you."

With a smile he walks into the afternoon heat.

Falling in Love

"Blessed are those who have not seen and yet have believed." John 20:29, NIV.

It's just a little photograph of two people standing under a tree. He has one hand on her shoulder while his other hand clasps the fingers at her side. They look so young and full of life. Sometimes it's hard for me to believe that the man pictured beside the beautiful girl is me.

I was about to leave my home in Tennessee for a job in California. We'd be separated, perhaps forever. Our dates had been fun, filled with adventure and surprises. But we weren't serious about each other. At least, I thought we weren't.

Several months later I sat on my bed in a house I shared with a medical student in Redlands, California. Beside me, on the table, propped up against my radio alarm clock, rested the little picture of the two smiling people. We'd been talking on the phone, bringing each other up-to-date on the happenings in our lives, sharing funny stories and serious thoughts.

She'd written long letters filled with hopes and dreams, some of which included me. Now, as I sat staring at the photograph, a strange and almost desperate feeling rose in my chest. She was so far away. Why? I needed her to be closer. I longed to see her face and hear her voice unencumbered by phone lines and photographs. I wanted her with me right now!

The idea seemed ridiculous at first. Yet the more it simmered in my mind, the more restless I became. I didn't want her to be in Tennessee. I wanted her in California, in Redlands, in my life. Could it be? Was it possible that I was in love with the girl in the photograph?

In May of that year I answered my own question with two little words: I do.

Anyone who tells me that they can't fall in love with Jesus because He's not around anymore has never stared at a photograph of someone who's mysteriously becoming special in their heart. And anyone who insists that it's impossible to build a relationship with the Creator because He's in heaven and they're on earth has never talked for hours on the telephone with someone who is becoming an important part of their lives. I fell in love while 2,000 miles separated me from the focus of my desires.

The Bible offers a beautiful portrait of the Saviour. Prayer acts as the powerful communication system between God and humanity. Perhaps it's time to put away doubt and uncertainty, stare at the picture, and make the call.

The Guide

Part 1

"You are my witnesses," declares the Lord. Isaiah 43:10, NIV.

One cold morning during a visit to the city of Jerusalem I got up before my parents and sister to discover that during the night a blanket of snow had fallen, covering the ground with soft, white folds. My teenage heart yearned for adventure, so I slipped into my warmest clothes, left the guestroom in which we were staying, and hurried to the Damascus Gate. The narrow streets of the old city waited peacefully in the half-light of dawn.

After exploring the hilltop that served as the foundation of Solomon's Temple centuries ago, I found myself roaming across the Kidron Valley and climbing the Mount of Olives. With deep reverence I passed through the front gate of the Garden of Gethsemane and stopped to rest beneath gnarled and twisted olive branches. My imagination was working overtime, trying to fill in the visual gaps separating me from the time of Christ when He walked the same paths.

Suddenly I heard footsteps. A man, probably in his early 20s, shuffled up beside me, a friendly smile lighting his weather-tanned face.

"Hello," I said in my best Arabic.

He nodded, then motioned for me to follow.

"Where are we going?" I asked. He just smiled and began walking, his worn boots crunching in the new-fallen snow.

We climbed the hill in silence. Each time I tried to begin a conversation, he'd just nod, pulling his threadbare coat closer about him as the cold wind whispered through the Kidron. *My Arabic must be pretty bad,* I thought to myself. I tried English. No luck. He simply smiled and continued leading me along the winding road.

Before long we came to a small church perched on the hillside. He pointed up at it and tilted his head questioningly.

Inside the little structure were display cases filled with handwritten portions of Scripture. I recognized names like Isaiah, Jeremiah, Psalms, and others. But it was the stranger's expression that captivated my attention. He'd run his hand along the smooth glass separating him from the sheets of faded parchment as if he was touching something of great value. Such reverence. Such deep affection for those ancient writings.

Apparently it wasn't the only stop he wanted us to make. After motioning for me to follow, we left the little building and began our climb once again. Where were we going? What was I supposed to see?

Soon we stood at the very top of the mountain opposite the city, gazing down at the walls encircling Jerusalem.

"It's beautiful," I gasped. "Look how the snow makes everything so clean and—"

The words caught in my throat. The man beside me was crying.

The Guide

Part 2

Show me your ways, O Lord, teach me your paths;
guide me in your truth and teach me. Psalm 25:4, NIV.

Tears trickled down the stranger's cheeks as he stood at my side, gazing at the ancient city. His eyes seemed filled with sorrow. I figured that something terrible must have happened to him within Jerusalem's cold stone walls.

"Why?" I asked softly. "Why are you crying?"

The stranger looked over at me and I saw that the anguish had passed, replaced by a tired and kindly smile. Once again he motioned for me to follow.

Next he led me to a small café in an old building by the edge of the road. The warmth inside felt good to my face and hands, and the dim recesses of the room provided a welcome relief from the early-morning brightness.

"I see you've met my brother," an older man with a thick Arabic accent called as I sat down near the window. "He's the best guide in Jerusalem. Been taking tourists up and down the Mount of Olives for years."

"But he doesn't ever say anything," I sighed. "Doesn't he know English at all?"

The older man walked to my table and took a seat across from me as my mysterious self-appointed guide busied himself preparing cups of hot chocolate at the counter. "You're not the first visitor to find that a bit puzzling," he said. "You see, my little brother doesn't talk because he can't. He's never said a single word. Doctors call it a birth defect. They say he'll never be able to speak. Not ever."

With a satisfied grin my guide placed a steaming cup before me and then hurried to the door. With a wave he was gone.

"Heading out to look for someone else to lead up the mountain," his brother announced with pride lifting his words. "Works from sunup to sundown."

"But," I protested, reaching into my pocket, "I didn't pay him yet."

"Wouldn't do any good to try," the man said, raising his hand. "He never asks for money. You see, my brother's a Christian and believes God wants him to spend his life showing visitors the beauties of the mountain. It's like his witness. His . . . silent witness."

Today, whenever I think of Jerusalem, I picture two men climbing the Mount of Olives. One is Jesus, the Son of God, walking the narrow paths, knowing full well He'll be betrayed and crucified by the very people He came to save.

The other is a kind, weather-worn stranger with a threadbare coat and friendly smile who demonstrates daily that the sacrifice of the first still changes lives today and brightens the way for anyone willing to experience the silence of redeeming love.

Regrets

I have seen all the things that are done under the sun; all of them
are meaningless, a chasing after the wind. Ecclesiastes 1:14, NIV.

It's an oft-repeated scene. The family gathers around the dying form of their patriarch, his body frail and spent. The man's old and knows he has only hours to live.

His has been an interesting life, filled with love and unselfish labor for others. He will be missed, but everyone in the family knows that our existence on earth is transient. All have accepted the inevitable.

The man thinks back over the years, reviewing the past, examining each detail, each turn, each decision. He has regrets, as most do. If he had the chance to live his life over, he'd make adjustments, some rather major.

Perhaps he wouldn't take that job on the coast or move to the big house in the valley. He'd spend more time with his children and less time trying to earn his way into more affluent neighborhoods.

Now he knows he'd treat the little annoyances of life differently. They weren't that important. Not really. And there were people he'd definitely keep off his friendship list.

They ended up hurting him and his family, causing them much pain with their ceaseless greed and selfishness.

Yes, he has regrets—many regrets. If he could do it over, he'd live a different life.

Jesus and the Father stand together at the gates of heaven saying goodbye. It's time. The moment They'd planned for, the moment They'd chosen when They laid the foundations of this earth, is now upon Them. Jesus is to travel to a dark, sinful world to be born as a baby in a sheep manger. He will grow up amid poverty and strife, be the focus of human hatred, be used, abused, taken advantage of, rejected, spat upon, and finally killed as a common criminal.

Both members of the Godhead know what His life will be like *before* it happens. All decisions and their consequences, all the painful twists and turns, all the unhappiness, fear, uncertainty, and doubt, stand revealed to Them now. Every cause for regret can be clearly seen and reviewed by Their powerful minds, yet They stay the course, They make no changes, They say goodbye.

Somewhere in the darkness a baby cries, and a young teenage mother holds Him close. The father, a man who must trust that the child in his wife's arms is in fact the Son of God, stands nearby, wishing he could find a more comfortable place in which to house his new little family. If only they'd left Nazareth a day earlier. If only they'd not lingered along the way. If only . . . if only . . . if only.

Father in heaven, help me to accept the decisions in my life that may later become regrets. Help me to live so focused on Your love and Your will, so centered on what's really important, so unconditionally willing to allow You full access to my thoughts and desires, that I'll have no time for regrets—only praise.

Thank You for showing me how.

In Jesus' name, amen.

Bottle Cap Salvation

How priceless is your unfailing love! Psalm 36:7, NIV.

They used to be friends. Now they're locked in a legal battle over who owns a bottle cap. Every so often in the United States a major soft drink manufacturer announces a contest with prizes ranging from free cases of their product to millions of dollars. It was one of those million-dollar campaigns that destroyed a friendship and provided a powerful echo of God's love.

A woman got thirsty one day and purchased a soft drink. She popped open the top and threw the cap in the garbage. Then she enjoyed the beverage inside the bottle.

A coworker, who remembered the cola contest under way, fished out the bottle top and looked to see if it had a message printed inside that would indicate that the owner of the cap was a winner. Sure enough, there was the announcement in living color!

When the thirsty woman discovered that "her" cap was worth a million dollars, she demanded it back.

"No way," countered her friend. "You threw it in the trash."

"Doesn't matter," she insisted. "It's still my cap."

"Not after you tossed it," reasoned her coworker. "I fished it out of the garbage. That makes it mine."

The two women are taking their battle to court, where lawyers will probably make more money than everyone else involved in the case. Each party claims ownership of the bottle cap. Both argue that the big prize should belong to her. Who will win? Who *should* win?

I know a lot of people who, like the thirsty woman, get out of life what they want and simply toss everything else, including God, aside. They forget that there's a contest going on, a great, cosmic struggle for the salvation of every individual. Perhaps they might even act as if they've already earned the salvation prize—attending church, helping the needy, even teaching a Sabbath or Sunday school class. But they've thrown away their chance at the ultimate reward by not recognizing the value of what God offers.

Then there's the friend, neighbor, or family member who picks up the promises that someone else has tossed aside and sees their value right away. They excitedly shout, "I've been saved. I've been saved!" They are the true winners.

So many people live their lives without the benefit of God's indwelling presence because they've rejected it. They've thrown away the prize.

In our world of sin we're all losers until we discover *and act upon* the beautiful reward God offers in His Holy Word. Knowing that the prize is there doesn't make us winners. Only when we recognize its true value and turn it in to the authority of heaven can we ever hope to enjoy its riches. And we must never, *never* let someone else claim what is ours.

Have you discovered the value of Jesus Christ? Tell your heavenly Father. Show Him the bottle cap. And get ready to accept the priceless reward of eternal life. It's yours not because you've tasted a portion of its bounty, but because you've recognized and acted upon its wondrous worth.

Sad Smile

Therefore my heart is glad, and my glory rejoiceth:
my flesh also shall rest in hope. Psalm 16:9.

I look at her eyes through the viewfinder of my camera. Sadness hides in her gentle smile. Such sadness.

She sits by the window where the light is good, waiting for me to adjust the focus and exposure so I can take her picture. My magazine editor expects photos with the article that I'm writing on what today's teenagers want to ask God most. But I've lost interest in cameras and photography for the moment. All I can think about is the question she raised.

Her words echo in my mind again and again like a distant bell. "Why did God allow my father to die? I loved him so much. We were best friends. Now he's gone. Why?"

I don't have an answer.

Oh, I can say something like "Because God knows best" or "Someday we'll understand." She's probably heard such words before. But to me those phrases are empty and even dangerous. They tend to portray God as a murderer, selectively ending lives for some cosmic purpose to which we're not privy. Such thinking forces us to start each morning wondering, "Is this the day God will take me or someone I love? Am I so weak or so bad that I'm not worth His life-sustaining power any longer?"

I don't want to worship a Being who takes moms and dads and children away from those they love. No! I believe in a God who *gives* life, who sustains it, who nurtures it for as long as possible. Evil may destroy for a time, but God will ultimately save forever. That's the Power to which I pray.

Slowly I press the shutter release. With a click my lens burns her image onto the film waiting in the dark recesses of my camera's mechanical body. I thank her, and then, with a wave, she's gone.

Later, alone in my home office, I sit staring at her photograph. It rests on my desk among the others. But I can't escape her eyes or forget her sad smile. And I feel guilty because I didn't have a ready answer.

Questions will haunt us for as long as we must live on our dying world. Sin isn't fair. It hurts for no reason at all. One day we're happy, the next we're sad. That's life.

It's not easy being a kid. Nor is it easy being an adult, either. We all have questions with no answers. But this much I know. Someday I'll take the girl in the picture by the hand and walk along streets made of gold. We'll find Jesus waiting in the shade of the tree of life. He'll smile when He sees us coming, because, standing beside Him, will be the girl's father, alive and happy.

We won't have to ask why. It just won't matter anymore.

NATURE

Arms

For the arms of the wicked shall be broken:
but the Lord upholdeth the righteous. Psalm 37:17.

Victor Berge felt something touch his left arm. While such an experience wouldn't have caused the man a moment of concern in a crowded elevator or busy sidewalk, Victor just happened to be 20 fathoms deep in the Pacific Ocean off the coast of Borneo. At this particular spot on earth the only creatures that would bother touching him had more than a friendly greeting in mind.

"I grabbed the knife from my belt and slashed out again and again," he later recalled. "That's when I felt the long, slimy arms beginning to encircle me, crawling all over my body like snakes."

His afternoon dive to search for pearls had suddenly turned into a life-and-death struggle with a giant octopus. "Two other arms took hold of my legs and pulled me with a jerk," he recalled, "almost throwing me down. I could see the whole mass of waving squirming appendages. I tried to cut my ankles free, but the creature continued to jerk me so violently that my head struck the inside of my helmet, almost knocking me out. I was afraid to pull my emergency line for fear that my air pipe and lifeline might get tangled in the jagged coral."

More arms seized the man as he continued to slash out with his knife, fighting to see through the black, inky fluid the animal kept squirting into the water. "The octopus has the weirdest, most terrifying eyes of any creature in the world," Victor insists. "The stare of the loathsome orbs decided it for me. No matter if my air pipe and lifeline did become snarled; nothing mattered now. I took hold of the line and gave four jerks, sending a signal to the surface, 'PULL ME UP NOW!'"

Victor's pearling partners in the support boat felt the desperate tugs and began to pull frantically on the line. But it didn't move. Something was holding their friend under the waves. The harder they pulled, the tighter the animal gripped his victim. In the violent tug-of-war the octopus proved the stronger.

Finally the men floating above lashed the line to the boat itself. As the next swell lifted the craft, the terrific strain produced by the sea broke the deadlock. When their friend surfaced, the astonished men saw the octopus still wrapped tightly about Victor. One dove into the ocean and quickly cut loose the hapless diver, who by now was totally unconscious. The diving party gently lifted Victor into the boat and hurried to shore, seeking medical attention.

Arms. The devil has lots of them. They creep serpent-like around us, enveloping us, dragging us into the darkness. But God isn't about to let us perish. Hearing our cry and feeling the pull of our prayers, He jumps into action. So begins a desperate tug-of-war with us as the prize.

Like Victor Berge, we can rejoice that God's arms are stronger and can lift us out of darkness into life.

Darkness

I will lead them in paths that they have not known:
I will make darkness light before them. Isaiah 42:16.

Caves can be fascinating places, filled with echoes of God's creative power. But they can also become chambers of horror as discovered by Hugh Monroe and Thurman Treadwell, two teens from Ada, Oklahoma. Thurman wanted to collect some frogs for biology class, and Hugh offered to go along.

They hiked into the Arbuckle Mountains and soon found a cave. Such geological features can be home to thousands of frogs. The two explorers quickly removed their clothes, slipped into their bathing suits, and headed into the inky blackness, flashlight in hand. Before long they arrived at a big pool of water and started across, swimming and wading their way along. Then suddenly the flashlight went out.

Anyone who has ever explored deep underground can tell you just how dark a cave can be. The two boys didn't know left from right or even up from down. "We've got to get out," one told the other. "No one knows where we are."

They began inching their way along, trying to retrace their steps. The only sound disturbing the utter silence was their labored breathing and the croaking of the very frogs they'd come to catch.

Minutes ticked into hours. Time and time again they'd slip into a pool of water not knowing if it was the same pool they'd visited before in their desperate search for freedom. Trying to figure out what to do next, they discussed the situation. Then they prayed, but wondered if God could hear them in such a dark and lonely place.

Back in town, friends became worried. Thurman and Hugh didn't come to supper that evening, or breakfast the next morning. Search parties fanned out through the mountains, but no one knew exactly where to look.

Finally, 48 hours after the boys had disappeared, one group found clothes at the entrance to a grotto. "They're inside," the search leader announced, but his tone didn't hold out much hope of finding them alive.

Into the darkness went the rescuers, calling repeatedly, shining their powerful flashlights into every nook and cranny of the cave. At long last they spotted the two boys huddled together in the darkness, terrified of every sound and even the approaching forms of their rescuers.

"I felt like running away and hiding when I saw them," Hugh recounted from a hospital bed. "Their shouts terrified us. I guess we were in pretty bad shape."

Does the call of God ever frighten you? Perhaps you've been lost in the inky blackness of sin for so long that even the promise of salvation terrifies you and sends you into hiding. In times like that, you need to know that God doesn't come to condemn, but to save. His voice brings with it new hope and energy for living. All you have to do is welcome His presence and allow Him to take you out of the darkness and into the light.

Duck Story

Part 1

I will put my law in their inward parts, and write it in their hearts;
and will be their God, and they shall be my people. Jeremiah 31:33.

Dorinda and I live on a hillside overlooking a peaceful West Virginia valley where clouds sometimes drift low among the tall oaks and pignut hickories, and wood thrush sing from deep within the shadows. Just behind the house is a wooded area filled with birds, squirrels, and bugs of every persuasion. At the base of the woods rests a little pond.

The small body of water hosts the usual inhabitants: frogs lullabying each other to sleep at night, fish splashing in the morning sun, a turtle or two perched atop a half-submerged log. There's even a water snake that glides by occasionally, searching for something to eat.

One warm spring day we were looking out over the placid waters when an idea surfaced in our minds. As beautiful as the pond was, something was missing—something with webbed feet and soft feathers. Something that could paddle across the ripples or fly among the clouds overhead. Something that quacked.

A quick call to our local farm supply store put wings to our dreams. "Yes, we can order just what you're looking for," the voice on the line assured us. "They'll arrive in about two weeks."

I glanced at my wife and grinned. That was the easy part.

When the big day finally arrived, we jumped into our car and drove to the little town of Berkeley Springs, six miles away.

"They sound hungry," the salesman behind the counter said. We lifted the lid and peeked inside. There, looking back at us, were 10 of the cutest, softest, wriggliest baby ducks we'd ever seen—all chirping, squawking, whistling, and scolding each other while trying their level best to get out of the box.

"Hold on there, guys," I said, carefully closing the lid. "We've gotta get you home first."

After paying for our purchase, we drove back to the house while listening to the constant commotion coming from the cardboard box in the back seat.

The 10 new members of our family were only 2 days old, but already they wanted to explore the world. However, we couldn't just set them free. Dangers waited at the pond for baby ducks. We could not ignore the possibility of foxes, snakes, raccoons, turtles, stray cats, and hungry dogs. As guardians of those innocent, vulnerable creatures, my wife and I had to protect them until they could learn to fend for themselves.

A certain Bible text took on particular significance during that time: "O Jerusalem, Jerusalem . . . how often I have longed to gather your children together, as a hen gathers her chicks under her wings, but you were not willing" (Matthew 23:37, NIV).

For now, the new arrivals would live safely under our wings.

"What if they drown?" I asked as I filled a basin with cool water from the old metal sink in the laundry room.

My wife, whose judgment I trust most of the time, shook her head. "They won't drown," she insisted. "They're ducks."

I looked at the tiny, furry creatures with their oversized beaks, legs, and feet. They were only 3 days old and had never seen enough water in which to swim. "Ducks like water," she continued, shaking her head as if to convince herself. "God made 'em that way."

"OK," I agreed reluctantly. "We'll give it a try. But if I have to do mouth-to-beak resuscitation on one of these little guys, it's your fault."

When the water level in the basin looked about right, I turned off the faucet and lifted one of the baby mallards away from the rest. "Don't be afraid," I told him. "It's just water and—"

The instant the chick caught sight of the cool, clear liquid, he jumped out of my hand and dove, headfirst, into the basin.

He was all over that tiny pool, swimming, diving, peeping, squeaking, flapping his tiny featherless wings and raising such a commotion that all the other ducks suddenly felt totally left out and almost jumped out of their apple box. One by one I lifted the remaining nine and placed them in the basin, thus creating a joyous madhouse of ducks.

Dorinda and I knelt with chins resting on the sink rim and watched the tumult with relief and satisfaction. Sometimes, it seems, our happiest moments come when we simply do what God programmed us to do. Ducks can swim. We can love.

Duck Story

Part 2

He shall cover thee with his feathers,
and under his wings shalt thou trust. Psalm 91:4.

As the 10 baby mallards grew, we noticed something interesting. Each had a distinct personality. Oh, they looked alike, made the same noises, sat and preened their delicate feathers exactly the same way. But there were differences.

Several were passive and kept to themselves, choosing secluded corners of the apple box in which to spend their time. Others showed definite signs of aggression, constantly mingling with the others, trying to grab attention or attempting to generate interest in some secret duck game known only to creatures of the wild.

Several enjoyed sitting in the sunlight streaming through the window while others sought out dark, quiet spots under the straw. A couple ducklings took many naps during the day. Others seemed to have an endless source of energy, keeping busy hour after hour.

All were mallards and had been born on the same day. But all were different.

Sometimes I look around my world and wish that everyone were like me. There'd be no arguments, no "creative differences," no misunderstandings to muddy the social waters. We'd all be of like mind, everyone striving for the same goals. Even the choice of restaurants would be a no-brainer.

But God doesn't do things by accident. His creative powers follow a logic that human minds can't seem to comprehend. He made us to be different for a reason.

I'm sure that in Eden those differences would have brought great joy and satisfaction to every earthly inhabitant. That was the plan. Then sin entered the human heart, and suddenly everyone's distinctiveness became an affront to our personalities, challenges to our choices. We began to notice the differences while ignoring the similarities. Pride and prejudice evolved right along with such damaging traits as dishonesty and greed. Somehow we started to believe that if someone is different from us, they're wrong.

God saw it coming and made some adjustments of His own. One writer penned it this way: "The Spirit of God is manifested in different ways upon different men" (Ellen G. White, in *Review and Herald,* May 5, 1896).

It was our job to love and care for our little family in spite of their differences. What a beautiful echo of God's love for us all. No matter what type of person you are, your heavenly Father has a special, one-of-a-kind love created just for you.

One bright summer day Dorinda and I decided it was time for our little friends to meet the great outdoors. We placed them gently in a cardboard box and carried them to the yard.

"OK, you guys," I said, opening the lid and tilting the box slightly so they could jump out. "Don't wander off too far." One by one they ventured over the lawn, mumbling softly to themselves.

If I could understand duck talk, I'm sure they were saying things like "Hey! What's this long green stuff? Smells nice. Look at these little yellow flowers growing out of the ground. Have you ever seen such hard rocks in all your life?" When they'd pause and gaze skyward, I could imagine they were saying, "Will you look at those big fluffy things up there? Where'd they come from? And check out this big bug. Hum. I wonder how it tastes?"

As they were waddling about exploring the soft earth and the wonders of our front yard, the dark, shadowy form of a hawk appeared in the distant sky, and its chilling call echoed across the valley floor. All 10 ducklings froze in their tracks. In the next split second they raced across the lawn to where my wife sat. Without a sound they dove under her legs and completely disappeared from view.

Dorinda gasped at the suddenness of their response to the predator. The animals in our care had never seen or heard a hawk before. But God had planted in their tiny minds what I can best describe as enmity against such a threat, an uncomfortableness whenever a predator came within shouting distance. All this took place before they were even born.

The shepherd David wrote, "You are my hiding place; you will protect me from trouble and surround me with songs of deliverance" (Psalm 32:7, NIV).

As children of the Creator, when temptations and dangers come, all we have to do is follow our instincts, allowing the powerful enmity planted in us in Eden to turn our feet from sin, and then run unashamed into God's arms.

Duck Story

Part 3

He leadeth me beside the still waters. Psalm 23:2.

Our ducks grew and grew, finally graduating from the basin in the sink to the plastic wading pool on the front porch. Their feathers began to fill out, replacing the soft down covering their bodies with a smooth, carefully preened and oiled coat of color.

When we'd go for our evening walks, they'd fall in behind us like well-trained soldiers, following us about the yard, tumbling over each other as they tried to keep up. A more curious bunch you'd never find. They felt it their sacred duty to explore every inch of the yard, every fallen log, every sweet-smelling flower.

Wing feathers sprouted and our little friends would stand in one spot and flap like crazy, sometimes lifting themselves off the ground a few inches. They resembled clumsy ballerinas scurrying across the grass, half walking, half flying, mostly stumbling.

One day one of them quacked. It surprised him as much as it did us. He looked around as if to say, "What was *that?*"

Often Dorinda and I would sit on our favorite bench in the backyard under the hickory tree and the ducklings would gather at our feet, tuck their heads under their wings, and fall asleep. We could well imagine such a scene prompting David to write,

"I will lie down and sleep in peace, for you alone, O Lord, make me dwell in safety" (Psalm 4:8, NIV).

There was still one place we hadn't taken our brood. As yet, they hadn't seen the pond. We wanted to make sure they could fly away from danger before we introduced them to their final home. After all, once they laid eyes on that peaceful body of water, they'd never come back to the yard again. Right?

"It's time," I announced one afternoon. The ducks had been with us for almost six weeks. They could fly short distances, although their landings left a lot to desire.

"All right, you guys," I called. "It's time for a change." They all looked up at me and nodded—at least, it seemed like they were nodding.

With heavy hearts Dorinda and I made our way along the forest path, ducks following obediently at our heels. We walked them right down to the shoreline, hand in hand, knowing that they'd never want to leave their beautiful new home.

When they saw the water, they stopped dead in their tracks and strained their necks, studying the sparkling waves, listening to all the mysterious new sounds drifting about. Then, as one, they sat down on the ground and refused to budge. No way were they going any farther!

My mouth dropped open. "It's a pond," I said, "not a stretch of molten lava. You're ducks. You're supposed to love ponds!"

Well, maybe *other* ducks. But those creatures stayed right where they were. I pleaded, begged, beseeched, threatened, and even tried to bribe them with a juicy lettuce leaf, but they wouldn't move one inch. I wonder if God ever gets frustrated with us. He knows what would make us happy, but we refuse to accept His loving invitation, because we fear things we don't understand.

At my feet sat 10 ducks who were afraid of a pond. Where had we gone wrong?

Duck Story

Part 4

Now therefore ye are no more strangers and foreigners,
but fellow-citizens with the saints, and of the household of God. Ephesians 2:19.

This was embarrassing! My wife and I stared at each other with disbelief and then hung our heads in shame. We'd raised 10 ducks who, it seemed, were scared half to death of a pond!

Down the country road from our house lived an 11-year-old girl named Dusty. She was very wise, as are all children of her age. When I explained my predicament to her, she just shrugged. "I know why they won't go in."

"You do?" I gasped.

"Yup. No one's ever taught them how to swim in a pond."

I blinked. "Wait a minute. You're not suggesting that I . . ."

She smiled.

"There's a snake in that pond!" I protested.

My young friend lifted her hands and gave me that you-adults-have-so-much-to-learn look. "You're all the daddy they've got."

If you'd walked past the little pond at the edge of our property on a certain summer day not long ago, you would have seen a curious sight. How many times have you had the pleasure of witnessing 10 half-grown ducks sitting on dry land watching a human swim?

Long ago a God came to a dark place where a serpent lived, to teach us how to survive in a world of sin. He did it because He loves us, because we were afraid, and because we couldn't learn any other way.

A few days later, returning from an overnight business trip, my wife and I discovered that our 10 ducks weren't waiting for us by the house. Nor were they hunting for bugs in the field or wandering about in the cool shadows of the forest. No, we found them swimming in the pond, acting as if that had been their home since birth.

God never intended for us to live in a world damaged by sin. It was His plan to allow us to grow up in an environment free from disease and guilt, devoid of evil distractions, empty of any type of threat to our joy and well-being.

But that's not the world we face today. Sin has altered God's perfect plan, leaving us strangers in a strange land, wanderers far from home. That's why He came to live among us, teaching us that even though evil surrounds us, we don't have to let it defeat us. Even in the presence of the serpent, we can survive and prosper, our spirits intact, our happiness tempered only for a while.

Ten little ducks swimming in a pond offered a powerful echo of the love God has for each one of us.

Duck Story

Part 5

*Are not two sparrows sold for a farthing? and one of them
shall not fall on the ground without your Father. Matthew 10:29.*

It wasn't long before our 10 little ducks weren't little anymore. We'd hear them through the woods quacking and splashing. Occasionally they'd even visit the house, sitting on the low retaining wall by the garage begging for a handout of lettuce or watermelon.

As their feathers filled in, we discovered we had three males and seven females, plump and happy, dressed in their shiny, colorful coats.

We developed a daily ritual. Each morning I'd get up and go to a back window of our two-story house and quack out a greeting that sounded more Donald than mallard. I'd hear our friends respond from the direction of the pond. Minutes later they'd come all in a line, waddling through the woods to their favorite perch on the retaining wall.

Dorinda and I would hurry down to feed them handfuls of cracked corn and sunflower seeds. When they'd eaten their fill, they'd take off with a wild fluttering of wings, circle the house a couple times, then head back to the pond, touching down amid a chorus of splashes and happy quacks.

Occasionally, while I was sitting in my second-floor office, I'd see dark forms streak by my window. They'd sweep out across the valley, exploring the air, exercising their newfound freedom, reveling in the joys of unrestrained flight.

One day while watching the group swim across the pond, I frowned and pointed. "Something's wrong," I told my wife. "See that female over there? She's having trouble keeping up with the rest."

Sure enough, one of our duck friends seemed to be struggling, as if she couldn't get her legs to work properly. "We'd better keep an eye on her," Dorinda suggested.

The next morning I stood by the retaining wall, waiting to greet the mallards as they emerged from the woods. One by one they waddled down the path, quacking softly. "Four, five, six, seven . . ." I counted to myself. "Eight, nine . . ."

I waited. And waited. Then the tenth duck appeared. My breath caught in my throat. She was stumbling, falling, one wing dragging helplessly on the ground, trying her best to join the others already waiting on the top of the wall.

Sudden tears stung my eyes as I realized that one of our friends was sick and dying. As I stood watching the heartbreaking scene, the Lord placed in my mind a Bible verse I'll never forget. In a voice only I could hear, He said, "If a man have an hundred sheep, and one of them be gone astray, doth he not leave the ninety and nine, and goeth into the mountains, and seeketh that which is gone astray?" (Matthew 18:12).

I had nine healthy ducks waiting to love me, but my whole attention was focused on the one duck who was suffering. At that moment I understood how Jesus could die for one sinner. And at that moment I realized just how much He cares for me.

We must never feel alone in the world, nor must we ever believe that God has forsaken us no matter how sick sin has made us, no matter how injured we've become from evil habits or unwise choices. Jesus sees our pain. He sees our stumbling and hears our cries and sobs with us.

Autumn sent a chill throughout the woodlands and pastures surrounding our country home. The leaves turned crimson and gold. Early-morning frost began to appear on the grasses as the sun moved ever southward, shortening the days.

The nine ducks at the pond seemed to grow restless, glancing more often at the sky, watching winged V's of geese and other waterfowl pass high overhead. Then one morning they were gone, leaving behind two people whose lives they'd touched in so many wonderful and profound ways.

The pond seemed lonely after that. Oh, we still had the frogs and turtles and the little water snake to keep us company, but even they were getting ready to disappear into hiding places far from the reach of winter storms to come.

Would our ducks return in the spring? Or would they follow new friends to distant waters, beginning again the cycle of birth, growth, and migration?

It's been several years now. Pairs of mallards have visited our pond on different occasions. Were they ours? We don't know. They didn't stay. Perhaps our little body of water isn't big enough for raising a family. Maybe they found lakes and rivers more to their liking far beyond the horizon. But we'll always look and listen, just in case others stop by to say hello. For, in their voices and their lives, we'll continue to catch glimpses of God's presence, and glorious echoes of His love.

Germ Warfare

And Jesus went about all the cities and villages, teaching in their synagogues,
and preaching the gospel of the kingdom, and healing
every sickness and every disease among the people. Matthew 9:35.

You find it on the front pages of the daily news or heralded from the screens of countless television sets. "Germ warfare threatens the world!" the announcer warns. "You'd better watch out."

What the well-groomed man or woman sitting behind the microphone fails to mention is that germ warfare has been around a long, long time. Such attacks began on the outskirts of Eden when Adam and Eve's bodies felt the first twinge of discomfort brought on by something we all recognize now as the common cold. How terrifying it must have been to the two humans who'd never experienced pain. That first sneeze must have frightened them completely.

Germs, and all their mutant brothers and sisters, came about by the same process that eventually turned green leaves to crimson and spirited away the remains of animals and people who succumbed over the centuries. The human race looked upon such events as unnatural and frightening. They served as constant reminders that Eden had been lost, that a new power ruled the world.

The past 100 years of earth's history has seen an upsurge in the use of biological elements as weapons. Every so often a foreign dictator or a band of terrorists threatens civilization with mass destruction through germ warfare. Warheads filled with such things as anthrax and other biological agents bring fear to our hearts and make us long for the safety and peace of heaven.

Even before Japan's subways became battlegrounds in this sobering brand of combat, mobs in Osaka terrified victims with a particularly frightening implement of war. No, not guns or explosives. Their weapon of choice was something they carried on their skins: leprosy. The maimed, misshapen robbers would go secretly through the night confronting people, demanding valuables at the threat of infection. No pistol or bomb was ever so effective.

Rubber-gloved police officers drenched in germ-killing chemicals finally apprehended the bandits. Disinfectant covered the guards, judges, prosecutors, and defendants alike at the trial. The verdict? Guilty. The sentence? Not jail, but total, inescapable quarantine.

Someday the devil, the undisputed master and creator of germ warfare, will stand trial for his unspeakable crimes against humanity. He'll face a judge and jury drenched in the protective love of heaven. His trial will be thorough, leaving no doubt in anyone's mind, including his. Then the verdict will echo across the universe. *Guilty as charged!* The sentence? Complete and everlasting isolation through total destruction.

No more will humanity cower at the thought of attack. No more will children have to react in alarm to the stories reported on the evening news. No more will hearts beat with the uncertain rhythms of fear. The deadly plague of sin will be vanquished forever.

Germ warfare is coming on a cosmic level. But with hope born of faith in the unalterable promises of God, we can eagerly await the outcome.

Heavenly Visions

Eye hath not seen, nor ear heard, neither have entered into
the heart of man, the things which God hath prepared
for them that love him. 1 Corinthians 2:9.

How's your imagination? Pretty active? If it is, then you're in great shape to dream about heaven. Harps and white clouds may be fine for some, but not us.

One of the most devastating lies Satan has propagated here on earth is that heaven isn't worth the effort. I know a young man who insists that nothing about it interests him. He seems perfectly satisfied to enjoy sin for a season and then sleep the eternal sleep of the unconverted. My heart breaks because he'll miss so much.

I believe that such narrow-mindedness stems from a lack of imagination. God gave us brains for reasons other than for inventing the wheel or manufacturing weapons of mass destruction. He wants us to use our gray matter to create a vision of heaven that's worth fighting for, worth sacrificing for, a vision that merits a few life-changing struggles. This should be clear to anyone who has ever taken a walk in the woods.

In nature we find a fading reflection of a glory that once was. We discover traces of a place the Bible calls Eden, a wondrous garden filled with perfection and the amazing handiwork of the Creator. Eden was a place not only of peace, but of exciting science and breathtaking discovery.

Imagine living in a world in which God's creative power has been unleashed while unfettered by the degradations of sin. Also consider that God has invited you to share in that power, adding your eager hands to the continuous development of that perfect world. Suddenly harps and clouds don't quite cut it.

You see, we were not designed to be mere *observers* of science and nature, but, through Adam and Eve, God created us to be *participants,* operating at the very heart of God's unlimited creative process. And all of that He will restore to us in heaven.

Do you like music? Imagine being able to play any instrument flawlessly after just a bit of inspiring practice.

Enjoy sports? Consider what a baseball or football game will be like if no one is suffering from injuries, sickness, or a desire to make a fool of you.

Are you into photography? Let your mind be a camera and gather images from the far-flung corners of the cosmos to share with friends and neighbors "back home."

Is cooking your passion? Heaven's produce won't be spoiled and our taste buds won't be diminished by thousands of years of sin and greasy foods.

Do you have an interest in zoology? In the earth made new, animals won't fear you. You can study them up close and personal. Everything that flies, crawls, hops, or scampers will consider you a dearest friend, not a threat to their survival.

The list of possibilities is endless, limited only by your imagination. To anyone who has a brain and chooses to use it, heaven will be paradise.

As a sample of things to come, take a walk in a woods.

Migration

I will instruct you and teach you in the way you should go;
I will counsel you and watch over you. Psalm 32:8, NIV.

Somewhere in South America a tree swallow awakens from a restless night's sleep. It's early in the year, and the warm air carries the heavy scent of blossoms and the promise of rain. All of nature rests comfortably amid the lush surroundings of the jungle. But something is wrong.

It's been like this for days now. The bird seems to be eating much more than usual, spending hours skimming the river for gnats and searching the blue skies above the treetops for larger bugs and the occasional moth. It can't seem to fill itself up.

And its flying has been faster lately, more urgent, as if the simple act of taking to the air attempted to meet some new need. Even the stars dotting the night sky have mysteriously taken on special meaning, their placement in the dark void becoming strangely familiar, even friendly. They'd always been there, but now they looked different.

The bird had noticed a growing restlessness in others throughout the flock. Some who'd been with the group all season had disappeared. One moment they were there. The next, they were gone, heading north as if responding to some distant summons.

North. To the tree swallow it wasn't a direction. It was a pull, a tug at its rapidly beating heart. Something was calling it to fly in the direction of certain stars, along selected mountain ranges, over particular rivers and valleys. On this beautiful morning the call grows stronger and stronger. Suddenly the bird becomes one of those who has left the flock.

It flies endlessly, knowing that it's on course but not knowing how. It's as if the creature has a map in its brain, a detailed description of when to turn, how high to soar, how long to follow specific features on the ground. One day, two days, three days—it's lost count. The bird just knows it needs to continue the journey, reaching for familiar stars, crossing familiar boundaries.

Then, suddenly, it lands. Everything around the bird says the journey is over. The tall tree rising from the field on its left, the forest behind, the mountain ridge across the valley—they all just feel right. The tree swallow folds its wings and rests. It's home.

I get up from my desk and look out the window of my second-floor home office. Work on the manuscript that glows on my computer screen has tired my eyes and made my fingers ache. It's a story about our journey to heaven, about how we sometimes get confused and don't know if we're on the right course.

Glancing at the nesting box perched high on a pole in front of the house, I see a small form resting proudly at the highest point, a thin, exhausted creature with green wing feathers and a white chest. It's back—the scout, the first of the flock. I look at the calendar. March 21. It was the same day last spring, and the spring before. Soon the others will follow.

Suddenly I know how we get to heaven. We trust the same voice that guides my little friend year after year for thousands of miles across two continents. Our journey begins with a growing restlessness amid comfortable surroundings and ends at the gates of glory.

The Gift

For the mountains shall depart, and the hills be removed;
but my kindness shall not depart from thee. Isaiah 54:10.

At first we thought it was a weed. But it looked kind of nice sitting there beside the retaining wall in front of the house. So we allowed it to grow. After all, a bush is a bush. Those of us who are horticulturally challenged will leave something that's actually surviving day after day even if it turns out to be an Amazonian man-eater.

My wife and I would walk by in the evening and see it growing, filling out, turning different shades of green, waving delicate leaves in greeting.

"What if it spreads nasty weed seeds all over the lawn?" Dorinda mused.

"What if it poisons the grass with some sort of toxic plant juice?" I wondered aloud.

But we left it to its own devising, enjoying each perfect stalk and bud as they grew higher and higher, thicker and thicker, greener and greener. It might kill us all, but it sure was pretty!

One evening we were surprised to see a collection of tiny flowers beginning to open on the two-and-a-half-foot-high bush. They had large round centers and dainty yellow leaves fanning around them in a delicate array. The next day an explosion of the most beautiful sunflowers we'd ever seen greeted us.

"A sunflower plant!" we gasped. "How'd that get here? We haven't planted sunflower seeds anywhere on the property. Oh sure, there are lots of them behind the house in the bird feeder, but—"

Then we understood. While *we* hadn't planted any, we'd certainly been feeding bags of the stuff to the chickadees, house finches, and chipmunks that swarmed the yard during the winter months. Apparently one of our feathered or furred friends had carried a remnant of some long-forgotten breakfast to the front of the house and dropped or buried it by the wall. When the summer sun warmed the soil, the little gift had grown up and provided us with a cheery, yellow-petaled thank-you. At least we liked to believe that was the reason for its existence.

Sometimes good deeds come back to us in the strangest places and in unfamiliar ways. Our generosity, our sacrifice, our caring attitude for someone else, may seem to go unnoticed by the world, leaving us to wonder if our efforts are worth the trouble. Children lovingly raised by Christian parents go astray. Acts of kindness end up misunderstood or even ignored. Long hours spent in service seem to have no perceptible impact.

Yet in a world damaged by sin but still loved by God, no tiny bit of service will remain unnoticed forever. That child may return before it's too late. Our kindness may change lives in ways we can't even imagine.

What we think is a weed may actually be a heartfelt thank-you under development. In God's time the rewards of servitude will blossom, adding a touch of happiness and beauty to our lives.

Simple Song

I will praise the Lord according to his righteousness:
and will sing praise to the name of the Lord most high. Psalm 7:17.

He's not what you'd consider a beautiful bird. The only significant feature separating him from the rest of the sparrow family is the little rusty cap that he wears perched atop his feathered head. Even his song lacks that special something that makes walks in the woods such a rewarding experience. He just warbles a single note in a monotonous, staccato stream.

One day I was out helping my wife water her tomato plants when we heard the flutter of wings and saw the little chipping sparrow land nearby. Then the hot summer afternoon air began to echo with his tiresome call. Again and again he sang his simple song, sounding more like an insect than a bird.

We stopped our watering and stood watching him, impressed not by the notes, but by the delivery. With each rendition, the little sparrow tilted back his rusty-capped head, opened his tiny beak, and sang as if he was the only bird on earth. His whole body vibrated with the effort.

If I didn't know any better, I'd think he was actually proud of the noise he made.

In his mind he wasn't a common sparrow announcing the boundaries of his territory. No sir! By some magic of imagination he'd become a wood thrush or a mockingbird, filling the humid air with melodies rich and varied. At times he'd pause, as if accepting thunderous applause from unseen admirers. Bowing timidly, he drank in their passionate accolades, then offered encore after encore, doing his level best to satisfy the insatiable desires of his hearers.

Do you sometimes get the uneasy feeling that your song, your life, isn't worth much? It doesn't produce the melodies you dream about making or consistently bring value and beauty to those around you. Sometimes the only song you can sing is a monotonous rendition filled with doubt and discouragement. Your verses become heavy with tiresome duties and deep disappointments, your choruses laden with frustration. Are there days or even weeks when you have a hard time just finding the notes?

When this happens, think about the lowly chipping sparrow and the pride he demonstrates with his simple song. To Christians, it should be enough that we can sing at all. As children of God we must come to realize that it's not lilting melodies or soul-stirring harmonies that catch our Saviour's ear. No. It's the effort, the spirit, and the dedication behind our performance that means the most to Him.

Keep singing, even if the sound doesn't match your own ideal. For when you place your heart and soul in each note, as far as God is concerned you're making exquisite music.

The Unwelcome Passenger

Be sober, be vigilant; because your adversary the devil,
as a roaring lion, walketh about, seeking whom he may devour. 1 Peter 5:8.

Many years ago a passenger airliner sliced through the calm air high above the English Channel on its way from Europe to London. The passengers amused themselves with books or conversation while the captain of the craft skillfully guided it along its predetermined route.

Suddenly a cry of alarm sounded at the back of the airplane, followed by shouts and screams. Heads turned and mouths dropped open. This wasn't supposed to happen, especially in the skies above the English Channel! Slowly the focus of everyone's terror walked up the aisle.

By the time the commotion reached the first-class section, total pandemonium reigned. Passengers clambered onto the backs of their seats. Babies cried; old people clung to each other.

Sensing that all wasn't well in his airplane, the captain opened the door separating the cockpit from the cabin. He froze. Standing not more than a dozen feet away was a full-grown Bengal tiger, tail twitching back and forth, powerful teeth bared, nose wrinkled in an ugly snarl. No, the pilot's training manual hadn't covered this particular airborne emergency.

One thought filled every mind: escape! But to where? They were high over the channel, flying along at a couple hundred miles an hour. They couldn't run or hide. The passengers had to sit there, huddled against the seats, while the tiger glared at them with hungry eyes.

Suddenly everyone heard a new voice above the shouting and screaming—a German voice as urgent as the others. It came from a man who ran up the aisle waving his arms, trying to get the beast's attention.

The tiger turned and attacked, mauling the would-be savior badly, but the man fought bravely, edging back through the plane to the open cage waiting in the baggage compartment. He'd faced the ferocious animal before. They were both part of a circus. But that didn't detract from the fact that it still was a struggle for survival, a battle of life and death. Meanwhile, the plane stayed to its course in the sky, approaching ever closer and closer to its destination and the safety waiting on the ground.

Sound familiar? The Bible describes a "roaring lion" stalking the aisle of spaceship earth. We can't run or hide. There's no place to go.

That's when we see a Man lifting His arms to face the beast, allowing Himself to be nailed to a cross. The lion attacks. The battle is intense. Who will win?

After the airplane landed in London, the passengers filed out, pale and shaken, followed by the bruised and bleeding animal custodian. He had placed the tiger back in its cage. The brave keeper had won.

So has our Saviour.

Two Seas

Can both fresh water and salt water
flow from the same spring? James 3:11, NIV.

Even from space the difference is clear. One enjoys the company of vineyards and rich fertile fields brimming with harvest. The other rests alone amid barren, sun-scarred hills and parched valleys.

Two seas form part of the eastern boundary of present-day Israel. The first has had many names: Sea of Kinneret, Lake of Gennesaret, and Sea of Tiberias. Gospel writers Matthew and Mark gave it a title any Christian will recognize: Sea of Galilee. Its fresh, sweet waters provided relief and refuge for the Saviour when He walked among humanity. Often He and His disciples would camp on its shores, enjoying the cool breezes that blew in with the waves. Even today fishermen, perhaps descendants of Peter, James, and John, ply the waters searching for yet another catch to fill their nets.

The Sea of Galilee eagerly accepts the melted snows from nearby mountains and drinks deeply from the freshwater springs that dot its shores. Then, without resistance, it adds its collected bounty to the flow of the Jordan River, helping to awaken barren lands downstream with its unrestrained benevolence.

About 80 miles south of the pristine shores of Galilee the waters so willfully offered by one sea enter a completely different world shaped by another. They become saturated with salt and bitumen, losing much of their purity through evaporation. The shores of the second sea provide little shelter from the unrelenting sun and no refreshment for body and soul. Vegetation and animal life struggle to survive. The blistering wind blows dusty and shrill.

The second sea has had several names as well. Past civilizations have labeled it Salt Sea or the Sea of the Arabah. Modern humanity provides a more descriptive title: the Dead Sea.

Like its beautiful cousin to the north, the Dead Sea receives fresh water not only from the Jordan River, but also from several springs hidden along its shores. But that's where the similarities end. This body of water takes, but does not give. No rivers flow south from its boundaries. The Dead Sea keeps its bounty to itself, hoarding its natural resources year after year, century after century. Because of this, the area surrounding the sea has lost its ability to produce vegetation. Tree roots find no sustenance below the surface of the soil. Flowers have no protection from the scorching sun. Grasses gather no nourishment from the parched earth. The sea has spread its death like a dry, crumbling blanket over the face of the land.

Israel has two seas. One creates life with its unselfish sharing of all that it has. The other smolders 1,300 feet below sea level, refusing to share itself with the land. One hosted the footsteps of the Saviour. The other drowns in its own blessings.

The Doctor Is In

Whosoever shall call on the name of the Lord shall be delivered. Joel 2:32.

On a recent Friday sundown walk my wife and I came upon a female wood duck unable to fly. A quick examination of the unfortunate bird revealed a bulging protrusion near her stomach. We recognized it as egg binding, a serious condition our favorite bird book reported as needing the immediate skills of a veterinarian.

As the sun slipped below the horizon, I hurriedly called the nearest vet listed in the phone book. Being a fan of James Herriot, the famous English animal doctor, I totally expected his American counterpart to answer my call amid a chorus of barking dogs. Tristan and Siegfried-type partners would be standing by, ready to lay gentle hands on our feathered friend.

"Our office hours are Monday through Friday, 9:00 to 5:00," the recording announced. I called the emergency number throughout the evening and finally got an answer. "I'm taking tomorrow off," the woman informed me firmly as if I'd just asked her to operate on an elephant. "I can look at the animal on Monday during regular business hours." She hurriedly suggested a few things that I might try, then hung up.

The next morning I began calling every animal clinic listed in the phone book. I got machine after machine. The one office that was open didn't handle wild ducks. "Only common household pets," the person told me politely.

Meanwhile, the duck was getting weaker and weaker. By Monday morning, when I hurried her to the closest clinic, she could hardly move. Hours later, she died.

"If you'd brought her in a few days earlier," the receptionist intoned sadly, "we could have saved her." She wasn't aware that that's exactly what I'd tried to do. But her boss and every other vet in the area wanted the weekend off.

All for taking a break from work myself, I'll be the first to champion the healing power of a relaxing weekend away from the office. But I wasn't asking anyone to hang out their shingle for the whole day, to turn their backs on family and friends in favor of my suffering wood duck. It was an egg-bound waterfowl. In skillful and experienced hands, treatment is straightforward and quick. Work the egg out without breaking it. Duck regains strength and flies south for the winter. Everyone goes home happy. However, on this particular weekend, no one responded. The animal died.

I'm glad God's clinic stays open year-round. He doesn't post hours, doesn't even own an answering machine, and refuses to work through uninformed receptionists. He's there, on call, ready and willing to touch my life with spiritual healing anytime I ask. To Him, the simplest request is a full-blown emergency complete with wailing sirens, clanging gurneys, and white-robed angels of mercy standing by ready to pounce on the problem with unrestrained eagerness and limitless skill.

Thank You, Jesus, for never closing me out.

SCIENCE

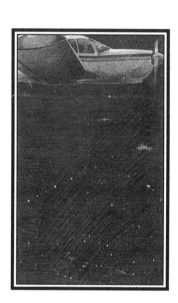

Lights

"You are the light of the world." Matthew 5:14, NIV.

My little airplane settles into its flight with a reassuring rumble. I sit at the controls making adjustments to radios and navigational instruments, selecting frequencies, twisting knobs, and saying goodbye to Albuquerque, New Mexico, departure control. Hundreds of miles stretch ahead of me before I reach my home port of Collegedale, Tennessee. It's just after midnight.

Behind where I'm sitting in my single-engine Cessna 210, stacked neatly from floor to ceiling, are cases of cassette tapes, each with a somewhat unusual label stamped on their faces. This night I have the rare privilege of carrying the recorded Word of God across half of the United States.

Late-night flights do something to young pilots, especially those with wild imaginations like mine. Here I am, drifting effortlessly two miles above the earth, looking down at tiny collections of lights that mark the position of sleeping towns and cities. Behind me, professionally recorded on cassette tapes, I carry the greatest message our world will ever hear, a message of hope and comfort. I realize that I have hidden in my little airplane the answer to everyone's problems. Everyone's.

After scanning the instruments, I allow my gaze to linger in the dark void below. That light way over there near the horizon is a farmhouse in which the farmer can't sleep and is lying in bed staring into the darkness, wondering if this season's harvest will earn enough to pay the bills. Or will he have to sell the land that's been in his family for five generations? Does he know that there's a God who will stand by his side no matter what happens?

Those lights down there mark a town in which lives a lonely widow who, after 10 years, still longs for her husband, still yearns for his touch, still aches to hear his voice and would give anything for a chance to prepare him just one more meal. Does she know that God sees her sorrow and offers comfort to her breaking heart?

That collection of lights gathered by the dark form of the river outline a prison in which an inmate on death row paces the floor, knowing that in two days he'll die at the hands of the state. He made a mistake—a horrible mistake—and must pay for his crime. But he accepts that fact and has made peace with the family of his victim. But now he wonders, *What lies beyond the grave? What waits for me after the injection?* Does he know that there's a God who forgives, who has prepared a place for those who've fallen into the web of sin and long to be free?

And that light over there. It shines from the window of a child who moans on a bed of sickness. The doctor prescribed medicine, but nothing seems to be helping. Mom and Dad stand by the bed, holding on to each other, wishing they could trade places with their fevered baby. Do they know about a God who understands what it's like to watch a son suffer, a God who is preparing a place where sickness, crying, and pain have been vanquished forever?

I glance back at the boxes of cassettes and fly on, eager to reach journey's end, eager to deliver my precious cargo, eager for the words they contain to filter back over the miles and touch all the lights of the night.

The Right Tool

He that believeth on me, the works that I do shall he do also. John 14:12.

The basement of our home has a little workshop filled with screwdrivers, hammers, and enough dangerous power tools to keep a big-city emergency room humming for days. Most of the items I purchased during times when I was experiencing illusions of grandeur.

"We need to fix that squeaky door," my wife announces.

"No problem," I answer with confidence. "But I'll need to buy a welding kit."

Oh, I *use* my collection of tools. Just the other day I made a nifty shelf for my office. That set of metric monkey wrenches really came in handy. And who would even think of repairing the riding mower without a trusty band saw waiting nearby?

Tools are such macho things. They're hard and shiny and tough. You can run over them with a truck and they'll still retain their usefulness, able to do incredible amounts of damage in the blink of an eye. I'm in awe of their raw, unbridled power.

But I've discovered that owning a tool, even the proper one for the job, isn't enough. Worse yet, *overusing* a tool, even the proper one, has the very real potential of doing more harm than good. Just ask my wife. She's seen the phenomenon demonstrated quite regularly around our home.

She and I once visited Colonial Williamsburg in Virginia and watched a group of skilled craftsmen fashion beautiful pieces of art, sturdy chairs, even sweet-sounding violins with tools that didn't plug in anywhere. They created flawless reproductions of objects made many years ago. I could spend a month of Sundays in my workshop surrounded by the latest and greatest electrically driven, diamond-bladed, computer-designed, and laser-forged tools and not even come close to their level of expertise. Why? Because it's not the tool that works the magic. It's the hand that guides the tool.

Anyone who has ever stood at the base of the pyramids in Egypt, watched a shuttle launch, gazed into the innards of a modern computer, or listened to the magic of a well-rehearsed symphony orchestra comes away from the experience with the undeniable realization that while tools may have limits, human imagination doesn't. Each requires the other to find its proper place in the world.

Our Christian duty is to echo God's love to others. We can fill our pockets with colorful brochures, purchase cutting-edge multimedia equipment, and utilize the latest communication techniques. Even more amazing, we can bounce truth off a satellite, invite the world to our new Web page, entertain with special effects, and even produce a virtual world filled with perfection. But it won't be the tools that impress in the long run. Searching souls will be moved only if our hearts and hands echo the caring concern of the Master Craftsman. If we want to reconstruct lives for eternity, God's love is the only right tool for the job.

Structure

*Behold, I build an house to the name of
the Lord my God, to dedicate it to him. 2 Chronicles 2:4.*

Several years ago my wife and I bought our first house. We spent a great deal of time locating the perfect property. Then we selected a company that makes modular homes. After building the basement, we gave the green light for work to begin on our humble two-story abode.

During construction we visited the factory each day, watching our house take shape in four sections. Rooms we'd only dreamed about until then assumed form. The kitchen, dining room, staircase, my office—each addition left us breathless with excitement.

Then the big day arrived. The construction company loaded our completed four-part palace onto truck beds and began its 50-mile journey from factory to foundation. You haven't lived until you've followed sections of your dream house down a freeway at 60 miles an hour.

One part of the building process made a deep impression on me. The man at the factory told us that we could make any changes to the blueprints we wanted as long as we left certain areas alone. "Those are structural," he told us, pointing at portions of the plans. "Can't touch 'em. Would weaken the house."

Today, as I sit in my cozy home office, I can't help thinking about how our little country home was built around unmovable, unchangeable rules of structure. The men and women who designed it understood those codes perfectly. They knew, literally, where to draw the line.

I'm free to add on a room, finish the basement, construct a deck, and make improvements because I know the structure is sound. I know what walls must stay, and which ones I can move.

Ever dreamed of changing your life? Want to add a new talent or adjust your career track, take on different responsibilities, or move off in untried, exciting directions? Before you begin construction, take a lesson from our man at the factory. Some things are structural.

Health is one of those areas. Whatever your plan of action, it must not affect that element unless you're willing to pay the price. Family is another. Your relationship with your spouse, commitment to God, dedication to heaven and the life waiting beyond the grave, keeping the Sabbath holy, returning an honest tithe, the Christian principles of honesty, hard work, and trustworthiness—they are all structural. They must stand unaltered by any decision you make.

Having lived in California where earthquakes tend to be common occurrences, I've subconsciously mapped out the safest spots in my house to which to run in case the ground begins to tremble. Guess what. Those "safe havens" coincide exactly with the unalterable areas the man at the factory indicated on the blueprints.

"That's structural," I hear him say. "Can't change 'em. Would weaken the house." Little did he know that he was echoing God's love to everyone who desires to build a new life around the powerful truths forming the framework of Christianity.

If I'm ever in doubt about where those areas in my life may be, I ask God for guidance. After all, He should know. He built me.

Hidden Miracles

*And a great multitude followed him, because they saw his
miracles which he did on them that were diseased. John 6:2.*

I have a little nephew whose middle name is the same as my first. We've both agreed that's
the moniker he prefers—at least until he's old enough to understand the difference.

Andrew Charles Mills experienced a terrible accident not long ago. While playing
at a fast-food restaurant, he slipped and hit his head. At first he cried. Then later he began
vomiting, and his frantic mom couldn't seem to keep him awake. Something terrible was
hiding beneath the swelling just behind his right ear.

That night, after a high-speed journey over icy roads to Children's Hospital in
Washington, D.C., Andrew Charles Mills underwent surgery to reduce the swelling in
his cranium. While doctors worked over him, he suffered a stroke, and part of who he
was died forever. Now, after months of therapy, he's doing OK, learning to live with
limitations he'll have to endure until Jesus comes.

During that horrific ordeal the question of miracles kept popping up. Many asked,
"Will God perform one for little Andrew?" Certainly family and friends offered enough
prayers to merit divine intervention. The moans and pleadings rising from that hospital

waiting room during the weekend would certainly move a loving God into quick and decisive action. After all, this wasn't some sinner who deserved to suffer, whose decadent lifestyle and selfish habits dictated a trip to the ER. No, it was just a little boy whose only sin might be an occasional act of disturbing the peace.

Alas, all the child did was survive. He experienced no sudden recovery. No team of physicians stood around shaking their heads wondering where the injury went. He didn't die, but that was all.

Instead, he underwent three emergency surgeries, spent a week hooked up to every life-support medical machine imaginable, had his brain rearranged, yet he still knows how to smile and is slowly learning to walk and talk again. If the accident had taken place 50 years ago, Andrew Charles Mills would be dead.

Sometimes we equate miracles with strange, unexplainable events: cancers suddenly vanishing, crippled airplanes landing intact, someone who was comatose for five years sitting up and asking for pizza. But how about the subtle, hidden miracles we experience every day? Medical breakthroughs show us how to live healthier, more productive lives. Air bags, shatter-resistant glass, plastic, shopping malls that ban smoking—these all contribute to our health and well-being in hidden yet miraculous ways.

Little Andrew was literally drowning in miracles that terrible weekend. Some arrived in the form of skilled surgeon hands and machines with dials and knobs that beeped continually. Years and years of experience and generations of knowledge came to bear on his tiny, fragile form. We all discovered to our joy and relief that, even before we asked, God had been preparing for Andrew's chance for recovery, using skills and knowledge developed before any of us had been born.

Someday, when he's old enough to understand, I'm going to tell Andrew about how we prayed for a miracle, and got more of them than we could count.

Guide Star

*Thou shalt guide me with thy counsel,
and afterward receive me to glory. Psalm 73:24.*

It hangs in space like a leaf adrift. It makes no sound, but only tiny movements ordered by technicians sitting in closed rooms many miles away. What it sees astounds us, for it can look beyond the present and gaze unblinking into galactic past.

I study the images it sends. My computer screen glows with portraits of exploding stars, distant solar systems, boiling clouds of gasses and cosmic debris. To me, the night sky will never be the same.

As I research further, one technical aspect of the image-gathering process catches my eye. I learn how the technicians aim the Hubble space telescope while it drifts in the dark void. What happens speaks to the very core of my own personal search for truth.

Commands sent spaceward from controllers on earth place an electronic grid over the Hubble's pointing display. Several previously identified and cataloged heavenly bodies serve as guide stars, making it possible to lock the big mirrored lens onto exact position while finer and finer adjustments take place. The more guide stars that the technicians can set into the grid, the more precise can be the search for distant views.

It seems that to discover the unknown, the Hubble space telescope must depend on the known.

Suddenly my endless probing for answers to life's most troubling questions comes into sharp focus. I'm forever searching reality, trying to discover meaning and purpose for my existence. Sometimes the journey seems hopeless, random, without cause or effect. All I see is never-ending space, filled with darkness and unknowns.

But, I muse, what if I chose a few guide stars to help me take aim at the answers? What if I placed the simple yet beautiful truths buried in the Bible over the grid of my life? More to the point, what would happen if I set the life of Jesus dead center over my pointing display, lock onto His sacrifice, and then gaze again into the void? Suddenly I know that the answers I've searched for so long will reveal themselves to me. Why? Because I'm permitting the Saviour to make those all-important final adjustments. I'm allowing Him to direct my sight with His love.

My computer screen flickers with visions unseen since Creation. Space is vast, unfathomable, mysterious. But the Hubble finds the faintest stars, the most distant galaxies, and captures images that sweep space and time aside like dust from a windowpane. No longer is its mirror blindly searching the universe. No. Night after night it records echoes of God's love because it knows where to look based on other recognized evidences of the Creator's power.

Men and machines can see amazing sights only when they allow their eyes to be directed by trusted and changeless guide stars.

Act of God

He that hath seen me hath seen the Father. John 14:9.

Attention, all aircraft. There's a little rain shower just north of the airport." The voice of Dallas-Fort Worth approach control sounds in the cockpit of Delta Flight 191 as it glides through the bright Texas sky.

"Looks like we're going to get the airplane washed," the copilot jokes, eyeing the rain falling silently up ahead. Passengers busy themselves with preparations for landing, stowing laptop computers and diaper bags in jammed overhead compartments. Flight attendants walk the aisles, collecting snack trays and soda cans. An air of expectancy fills the cabin. The long flight is about over.

The landing gear drops from the belly of the airplane as giant flaps grind into position behind the wings. Up ahead the runway stretches across the flat landscape, ready to receive the approaching aircraft.

Flight 191 slips beneath a towering cumulus cloud, and the travelers feel a slight buffet run the length of the cabin. What happens next, as reported by the National Transportation Safety Bureau, is an "atmospheric disturbance, which can be described as severe and localized." Powerful downdrafts and metal-tearing updrafts grip the airliner like a dog fastens onto a bone. The captain fights for control, but the forces of nature prove too much. He and his crew have themselves become passengers in the final moments of the journey. Flight 191 doesn't land. It crashes, killing 135 people.

Friends and family of lost loved ones turn tear-stained faces skyward, asking *why?* Reaching no conclusion, many label the calamity as simply an act of God.

An act of God? Could it be? For centuries human beings have tagged unexplained tragedies, violent natural phenomenon, and mysterious deaths as acts of God. Even less severe events cause fingers to point in heaven's direction. An illness becomes "a punishment." Some Christians label hard times as a spiritual "test." With the passing of a loved one, the phrase "it was God's will" is sure to rise from the lips of at least one well-meaning mourner. God becomes a scapegoat, a target for grief's unrelenting search for blame.

Does God lurk behind every unknown reason for tragedy? Is this the way He acts?

The Creator kneels on the riverbank, hands forming man from the mud. He breathes into the lifeless sculpture. That's an act of God.

We see the Son suspended on the cross, suffering for the sins of earth. That's an act of God. A stone rolls from a tomb, revealing a risen Saviour. That's an act of God.

Today, we watch as Scripture transforms a life. A marriage survives heartbreaking challenges. The Holy Spirit's power conquers deadly habits. They are all acts of God.

Someday those who endure to the end, who turn a deaf ear to Satan's lies, who stand on the foundation of Bible truth, will live where God lives. Heaven's redeemed will find peace at last and live forever as a result of earth's final and most glorious act of God.

The C Word

And ye shall know the truth, and the truth shall make you free. John 8:32.

Satan hates God, a fact that shouldn't come as a big surprise to anyone. Because of this well-known fact, we shouldn't be shocked at the lengths to which evil stoops to undermine the truth about the Almighty.

Recently my mother went to her doctor for some tests—something you do often when you're pushing 70. Needles pricked, machines whirled, computers hummed, and lab technicians gazed into microscopes. Before long, someone called my parents into the office to hear the results.

"Looks pretty good," the doctor said, eyeing my mother's CAT scan on his wall-mounted light box. He leaned forward for a better look. So did my mom and dad.

"There's a little scarring here," the physician stated as his pencil crept along the glowing image. "This is nothing. And this is nothing. This is cancer. This is nothing. And this is cancer."

The hearts of both my parents stopped mid-beat. They looked at each other, unable to speak. The doctor had said the C word . . . twice, without explanation.

Sensing their anguish, the man smiled. "Oh, those tumors are slow developers," he said, pointing at the smudges on the scan. "You'll die of old age long before they become a problem. Besides, even if they do act up, we can zap 'em with radiation. They're really nothing to be concerned about."

Two extremely relieved people called me later with the report and the story of their trauma.

What that doctor did through insensitivity Satan does by design. In describing our heavenly Father, he tosses out words like *judgment, hell,* and *death.* "God will judge you worthless," he taunts, "and bring about your untimely death. Then He'll throw you into an ever-burning hell!"

The doctor who frightened my parents that day in his office understood cancer far better than his patient. He knew that not all outbreaks of the dreaded disease cause immediate suffering and death. His experience had shown him, time and time again, that medical science can stop many forms of cancer completely. So when he mumbled, "This is cancer . . . this is cancer," he wasn't trying to cause a coronary in my parents. He was just stating a fact that, to him, was harmless.

But Satan is different. When he speaks, he purposely hides the real truth behind his words. He's trying to frighten us. And he succeeds with devastating regularity as demonstrated by the misconceptions about God heralded from churches, synagogues, and mosques around the world. We hear of a cold, vengeful Deity who delights in causing suffering for those who aren't good enough, penitent enough, or even rich enough.

In the pages of the Bible, however, we discover a completely different God, a Being who loves and forgives and saves, a Shepherd searching endlessly for lost sheep. We also find that judgment secures our salvation, hell is a result of *our* choices, not God's, and final victory swallows up even death.

If you want to know the truth about God, stand at the foot of the cross. That's where you'll meet Him. And that's where the lies and innuendos of Satan vanish.

PRC96-01a

The heavens declare the glory of God;
and the firmament sheweth his handiwork. Psalm 19:1.

For centuries human beings have shared a passion that seems to grow stronger with time. On any clear night, when the moon is new and the air is free of clouds and pollution, you'll find the faithful staring heavenward through handmade telescopes, expensive store-bought instruments, or even binoculars. What's the fascination? Stars.

Of course, the word *star* doesn't begin to cover what these nocturnal sky-gazers find so galvanizing high overhead. They're searching for planets, constellations, galaxies, clusters, nebulas, novas, pulsars, and even black holes. While they work, they speak in whispers, exchanging comments sprinkled with numbered brightness levels and orders of magnitude. Earthly distances pale in comparison to the unimaginable spaces through which they roam.

The late twentieth century offered a giant step forward in the star-studying community with the launch and deployment of an instrument named after American astronomer Edward P. Hubble. The Hubble space telescope has rewritten every book on the subject of celestial exploration.

119

In January 1996 the scientists controlling this amazing piece of technology looked about the heavens, searching for a new area to explore. Finding a dark spot billions of light-years away, they trained the Hubble's lens in that direction and began making long exposures, wondering what they'd find. They labeled the results Deep Field PRC96–01a.

For several nights in a row they left the unblinking eye of the instrument staring into the emptiness of space, allowing the sensors on board to register whatever light might be hiding in the shadows. This area of space had always been a mystery, filled with darkness, seemingly empty.

At last the long exposures ended and the command went up to transmit whatever data had been collected to computers waiting on earth. Astronomers watched as thin lines painted by the cathode-ray tubes began to sweep across their viewing screen. Was there anything out there? Had they been looking at the very edge of the universe, beyond which not even God ventured?

A gasp rose among the gathered scientists as the screen finally revealed its image in vivid detail. There, stretching endlessly into the distant eons of time and space, floated galaxy after galaxy, star system after star system, spinning, shining, and drifting through infinity. What some had considered an empty, featureless corner of the universe was, in fact, filled with vivid demonstrations of God's creative power.

In that one search of the heavens the Hubble space telescope reinforced a simple fact: God's presence can be seen everywhere—in the brilliance of the sun and within the dark cold confines of distant galaxies. He's found in places where no other life exists. And He's also found in your heart, and in mine.

O Lord, we've only begun to learn of You, of Your infinite grace and forgiveness. Please reveal Yourself in the dark spaces of our hearts. Teach us to recognize Your comings and Your goings. And whenever we gaze up into Your starry heaven, remind us of Your presence and Your love.

Spicy Christian

"You are the salt of the earth." Matthew 5:13, NIV.

He called us a chemical—sodium chloride, to be exact. But when Jesus uttered the above words, He had something important to teach us. To Him, salt represented a lot more than a spice. It symbolized life.

The English term *salary* comes from the word *salarium,* meaning "a soldier's money allowance for salt." The Latin term refers to the salt allotment issued to members of the Roman armed forces. In ancient times governments paid warriors with salt.

Used for millennia as a seasoning agent and food preserver, salt also found service in Greek, Roman, Hebrew, and Christian religious rites. So when Jesus identified us by that name, He had much to tell us.

Notice that He didn't say we are *like* salt. He said we *are* salt. The very fact that we have chosen to live our lives with Christ as the central theme means we've become the very seasoning our world needs most. Flavoring the lives of others with our presence, we preserve dignity and saneness in a civilization driven mad by sin. We cause irritation and then healing to the emotional wounds suffered by friends and neighbors who've fallen victim to selfishness, greed, and rebellion.

One day as Jesus walked beside the Sea of Galilee He saw some weary fishermen guiding their empty boat toward shore. He'd been around the region long enough to know that an empty boat in the morning was not a good sign. "Throw your nets to the other side," He called, His voice echoing over the waves.

Galilean fishermen weren't used to taking orders, especially from a stranger. They were an independent, somewhat rough around the edges type of people. On this particular morning they must have reasoned that because they'd tried everything else, what would it hurt to follow a somewhat curious suggestion. With a sigh they obeyed and wearily lowered their nets one more time.

Immediately they felt a reassuring tug. The stranger had guided them to the catch that would fill their stomachs and those of family members, neighbors, and friends as well. Later Jesus told several of the tough, weatherworn men that He needed someone to help Him catch an even bigger prize. When asked what He meant, the stranger simply said, "I need fishers of men." He was asking them to flavor the lives of others just as He had provided spice to theirs.

Salt flavors and preserves whatever it touches. Its effects are immediate and long-lasting. When we align our lives with Christ, when we choose to make His ways our ways, His standards our standards, we become transformed into something wonderful. We become salt, flavoring the world, preserving hope, and adding value and worth to the lives we touch.

If something isn't "salty," it isn't salt. In other words, salt cannot lose its taste. If it does, it's no longer salt. That's what Jesus was referring to when He stated, "If the salt loses its saltiness, how can it be made salty again? It is no longer good for anything, except to be thrown out and trampled by men" (Matthew 5:13, NIV).

Christians need not worry. God's presence in our hearts keeps the salt salty, and allows us the privilege of flavoring lives every day.

Medical Missionary

A merry heart doeth good like a medicine:
but a broken spirit drieth the bones. Proverbs 17:22.

Early in the spring of 1865 the commander of Union forces, General Ulysses S. Grant, lay in his tent nursing a blinding headache when a message arrived stating that the leader of the Confederate army, General Robert E. Lee, wanted to discuss terms for surrender. Grant later wrote that his headache vanished without a trace.

Medical science has many documented cases in which physical ailments, everything from heart trouble to asthma, have suddenly and unexplainably disappeared when dangerous or troubling situations ceased.

A young wife stares out the window as a blizzard batters the house. Her husband and children should have been home hours ago. Now it's almost midnight and still no word. She paces the floor, stomach aching, hands trembling, barely able to breathe. Then she hears the garage door open and sees the faces of her children peering out of the car through the blowing snow. They're home! Suddenly there's nothing wrong with her stomach and hands. She can breathe effortlessly and deeply. Sleep, something she couldn't imagine attempting moments before, seems inviting again.

Christ understood the vital connection between the human mind and body. His touch transformed both. He'd kneel at the side of a suffering man or woman and whisper that their sins were forgiven. That declaration alone brought immediate healing to many. People often heard Him say, "Your faith has made you whole." That's mind over body.

God calls all Christians to become medical missionaries of sorts. He asks us to go among the hurting even though we haven't taken courses at medical schools or sat for the many exams necessary to practice as a physician. All He requires of us is that we try to develop an acute awareness of the human mind and how it affects the body.

Many of the physical problems plaguing society today stem from guilt. When a life disregards divine law, when hearts turn cold with selfishness, hatred, and greed, the body suffers terribly. Ulcers, migraines, heart palpitations, even cancer itself, can overcome an immune system weakened by bad choices and unhealthy habits. The New Testament book of Revelation reports that in the last days human hearts will fail from *fear.*

All of these diseases, all of the painful ailments generated by the incredible interaction between a healthy body and a sickened mind, don't have to occur. We hold the antidote. Each of us has in our hands the formula for bringing healing to a troubled world. God calls us to visit the sick, the afflicted, and the sorrowing with a message of hope and for-giveness. He asks us to carry His touch to those suffering the results of sin in their lives.

The emergency room is full. We're on call. It's time to get to work.

A Picture of God

For now we see through a glass, darkly;
but then face to face. 1 Corinthians 13:12.

When I was a child a playmate told me that God lived in the clouds. From that moment on, every time a storm rumbled across the sky or lightning sparkled in the distance, I concluded that my heavenly Father was angry at me. I'd run and hide, hoping that He'd get over His unhappiness and allow the sun to shine again.

Then people told me that God wanted to live in my heart. All I had to do was invite Him in. This I did with great solemnity. But from time to time I'd do something foolish and figure that God had probably moved out in disgust. I really couldn't blame Him. Who'd want to live in an imperfect heart?

On those rare occasions when I did something noble or good, I'd glance at the mirror and grin with satisfaction. "I'm not such a bad home for God," I'd say to myself.

Maturity brings a degree of understanding to all children. At long last I fully understood what others were trying to tell me. God wants us to think and act *as if* He were living inside us, controlling our actions, guiding our thoughts. He *made* the clouds and little boys, too. That's the real truth of His presence. But with these realizations came a growing longing for an even deeper understanding of God's nature. I wanted to paint, as it were, a picture of Him to hang in the gallery of my life.

Have you ever felt that need? Have you ever wondered what it would take to re-create an image of God in your life? Allow me to share a few suggestions.

First, start with a clean white canvas, because God is sinless and perfect. Our easel must be strong, for God is our foundation. We purchase the best pigments, since God always provides what's best for us. Our brushes should be made from the finest materials, for God can be painted only from purity of thought and action.

Now we begin by sketching an outline of our hopes and dreams, smoothing subtle shadows of doubt into bold lines of victory. This forms the background of our masterpiece.

The face of Christ appears next as we trace the eyes that lovingly watch our every move, the ears that hear our every cry, the lips that speak words only we can understand. Next we form the hands that felt the nails, the feet that run to our aid, and arms that long to hold us.

If our paints dry out, we wet them with our tears. It makes the colors brighter. Finally, we frame our picture using rough, timeworn wood from the cross.

When we hang our masterpiece, we notice a lone Figure standing before it. He looks intently at the colors and studies every line. "Well done," He says. "Enter now into the joy of your Lord."

With thanksgiving we fall at the feet of the Master Artist. And with songs of gladness, we leave our brushes behind.

The Voice

*Now therefore, if ye will obey my voice indeed,
and keep my covenant, then ye shall be a peculiar treasure
unto me above all people: for all the earth is mine. Exodus 19:5.*

Sunlight poured into the cockpit and illuminated the clouds below with a brilliant glow. If circumstances had been different, the view from my lofty perch would have stirred my heart with amazement and gratitude. But at the moment I wasn't thinking about the beauty of flight and the grand vistas it offered. I was concentrating on survival.

The airplane had been built three years before I was born. However, unless I came up with a plan of action fast, we'd end our careers together in a smoldering hole in Tennessee.

The flight had started out routinely enough. My job was to follow my boss and his airplane from Chattanooga to Texas, depending on his navigational instruments and radios to guide us both to the man who'd purchased the Beech Bonanza I was flying. The instruments in my old airplane didn't work, at least not dependably.

We'd departed Lovell Field as a flight of two and had been cleared to visual conditions on top of the heavy overcast. But somehow I'd lost sight of my leader and was now sailing serenely over an ocean of billowy clouds without any way of knowing where I

127

was and where I should be going. I also knew that solid weather below stretched farther than my tank of gas would allow me to travel.

After spending more time trying in vain to catch sight of my boss's aircraft, I knew the situation was hopeless. There was only one thing to do. I dialed in the international distress code on my transponder and flipped on the only communication device in the panel: an old outdated radio with big knobs and faded numbers. "Mayday, Mayday," I transmitted into the blind, giving my aircraft registration number. "Does anyone hear this? Over?" Only static and the roar of the engine answered me. I repeated my call, asking if anyone on the ground or in the air was receiving my transmission.

Nothing.

Then a voice crackled over the speaker. "Bonanza, this is Nashville approach. What is your position?"

Someone had heard! A person I didn't even know had received my call and was trying to make contact with me. I offered where I thought I was, shouting into the ancient microphone held tightly in my hands, and then waited. I knew that men and women in darkened rooms many miles away were searching their radar screens, trying to locate the tiny blip that represented my little airplane and its transponder signal.

"Turn left," the voice crackled into the speaker, "and then turn right to help us find you."

I obeyed, watching the world spin slowly below my outstretched wings. Then came the call I'd been longing to hear. "Bonanza, you are radar contact 68 miles southwest of Nashville. Turn right to a heading of zero two zero and prepare for a precision radar approach to the airport. Stay on this emergency frequency for the remainder of the flight. Airspace has been cleared for you. You need not respond to these transmissions. Descend and maintain 4,000 feet."

Later, sitting in my airplane parked safely on the ramp of the big Nashville airport, I listened to the engine cool and watched the ice drip slowly from my wings. The voice had found me. It had guided me and saved me. But I'd had to ask for help. I'd had to confess that I was lost and didn't know my way home.

I was alive because I'd trusted the voice and obeyed its every command.

Latent Images

Let this mind be in you, which was also in Christ Jesus. Philippians 2:5.

You press the shutter release on your camera and hear a soft click. Then the smiles plastered across the faces of your relatives unfreeze as bodies relax and conversations continue. It's over in an instant. Yet every person sitting or standing before you has just been captured, their images kidnapped.

What happens during the next few days repeats itself millions of times yearly around the world. When you reach the last exposure, you rewind and remove the film from your camera. If you were to examine the roll, you'd find nothing—no smiles, no Christmas decorations, no breathtaking vistas from your vacation. Film fresh from your camera gives up none of its secrets. But don't worry; that great shot of Grandpa Milton eating a watermelon, last Monday afternoon's office party, or the wonderful moment when a certain someone turned to you and smiled while the two of you were walking along the beach do exist in all of their colorful, properly focused beauty. They just require a little help to become visible.

"We'll have them ready in about an hour," the clerk at the photo store tells you. Then the person behind the counter walks away with your precious roll of film and heads for a machine humming in the corner. A technician feeds your priceless, one-of-a-kind memories into a light-tight device that drags the film through a series of liquid chemicals designed to do what the human eye can't—change the invisible into the visible.

The images you worked so hard to capture are right there on the film. Uncle Harry blowing out his birthday candles, Grandma driving down the sidewalk in her new golf cart, little Ellen taking her first steps, brother Carl water-skiing on just one ski, your wife's prizewinning tomatoes—they're all there, waiting to respond to the chemicals, waiting to become what you remembered, waiting to thrill your heart once again. They just need to be developed.

A long time ago in Eden God placed in the hearts of earth's first inhabitants a roll of film. Oh, it's not really film. It's something much more powerful. The Creator called it *enmity*. After Adam and Eve ate the forbidden fruit, God said, "And I will put enmity between thee and the woman, and between thy seed and her seed" (Genesis 3:15). Most Bible scholars agree that what God placed in their hearts was an uncomfortableness or repulsion from sin. But I think it involves more than that. I believe He tucked inside Adam and Eve, and all future generations, latent images of His love, images that would become recognizable only as we developed patience, forgiveness, and the ability to accept the frailty of others.

Have you ever experienced trying times and come away from those encounters with a deeper, clearer understanding of God and His love? Have you ever discovered new insights just in time to apply them to challenges you face? You're slowly developing that divine "roll of film" in your life, seeing for the first time echoes of God's love that have remained invisible to you for so long.

Latent images. Timeless elements of photography and salvation.

Warrior at the Door

Seek him that maketh the seven stars and Orion,
and turneth the shadow of death into the morning. Amos 5:8.

According to Greek mythology, a mighty warrior guards the front door of my future home.

A Christian writer who has earned my lifelong respect, Ellen G. White, suggests that when Jesus comes the second time He will pass through a certain portion of space during His earthward journey. She wrote the following insight: "Dark, heavy clouds came up and clashed against each other. The atmosphere parted and rolled back; then we could look up through the open space in Orion, whence came the voice of God. The Holy City will come down through that open space" *(Early Writings,* p. 41).

Living in the country offers many benefits, not the least of which is the pleasure of seeing the night sky as God intended, filled with stars instead of streetlights. Our house in West Virginia faces east. Every autumn when the leaves turn from green to gold, a familiar visitor rises majestically over the ridge forming the distant horizon. I look for him, and when he appears, my heart skips a beat, for I like to believe that I'm gazing in the direction of my eternal home. The fact that there's a fabled Greek god guarding the way only adds to its beauty.

According to ancient storytellers, Poseidon, god of the sea, and Euryale, an unsavory ocean creature, married and had a son named Orion. The child grew up and fell in love with a comely maiden called Merope. But her father, Oenopion, refused to allow them to marry. Understandably, it made the young suitor angry, and he tried to get Merope through force. Well, Oenopion wasn't pleased at all and, with the aid of another god, put poor Orion into a deep sleep, then blinded him! When he awoke and discovered that he couldn't see, Orion consulted an oracle, who told him, "If you go to the east and allow the rays of the rising sun to fall on your eyes, you'll regain your sight." It worked! Able to see again, Orion moved to the island of Crete, where he worked as a hunter for the goddess Artemis.

Everything went along fine until Aurora, goddess of the dawn, took a shine to the young huntsman. Unfortunately, during a fit of jealous rage Artemis killed her handsome employee and placed him in the heavens as a constellation.

Greek gods lived some pretty rough lives.

So, it seems, do real ones. One day a virgin named Mary miraculously gave birth to a God she called Jesus. This Divine Visitor from the far reaches of the universe grew up amid poverty and mistrust, endured endless persecution for preaching peace and for-giveness, was sold out for 30 pieces of silver, and ended up nailed to a Roman cross. After spending three days in a tomb He then rose from the dead. He was despised, re-jected, lied about, scorned, made fun of, laughed at, beat up, and murdered. But through all that, He continued to preach a single message—heaven waits for all who willingly ac-cept His righteousness.

The Greeks were right. A warrior does guard the doorway to heaven. But the real God who stands watch isn't Orion. His name is Jesus.

Virtual Salvation

"Well done, good and faithful servant! You have been faithful with
a few things; I will put you in charge of many things.
Come and share your master's happiness!" Matthew 25:21, NIV.

Dr. Ben Carson's knife cut deep into the child's flesh, leaving in its wake a widening gap of muscle and tissue. The stakes were high, and the simplest blunder could be deadly. On the table lay not one but two patients, twin boys born 11 months earlier. They'd entered the world physically joined in such a way that neither had ever been able to crawl independently.

Many prayers had been spoken prior to the surgery, and even now nurses offered praise to the God who'd created the human body and had willingly promised to guide the surgeon's hands as they worked.

What made this particular operation unique was the fact that Dr. Carson, a well-known Christian neurosurgeon, had performed the exact procedure before in virtual reality. After the 28-hour operation ended successfully, he explained to reporters that during a visit to Japan he'd placed goggles over his eyes and had seen a detailed three-dimensional image of the same Siamese twins using data gathered by magnetic resonance imaging (MRI) and CAT scan technologies. The computer program called Virtual Workbench had allowed him to cut, explore, even travel directly into the surgery zone as if he'd become a blood cell himself. He'd experienced a dress rehearsal of sorts, an opportunity that enabled him to work quickly and efficiently later in Zambia, where the real operation took place.

The procedure was a great success. Two brothers whose bodies had been permanently linked before birth could now live the rest of their lives independently.

Their story is not unique. We've all been born securely fastened to a power not of our choosing. It stifles our potential, reduces our effectiveness, and hinders our every move. Then the Creator invites us to experience a new birth within the virtual reality of His grace. We slip on the goggles of faith and suddenly see solutions not evident before. We make cuts, explore our future, and even learn to crawl unencumbered by evil's persistent presence.

In this dress rehearsal for heaven we clearly see the damage in our lives, the places where the blood vessels have been severed and where the muscle and tissue forming our connection with God are weak. After each soul-searching session with the Master Physician, we can step back into the real world and get to work, repairing the damage brought about by generations of sin, suturing broken relationships, mending bruised and bleeding emotions.

In this virtual spiritual world we also catch a glimpse of heaven. Our hearts begin to yearn for our home with Jesus. We've seen the future and experienced the glory that awaits those who build permanent partnerships with God.

Someday the virtual world we now experience only with God's help will become a reality. We won't need those goggles anymore. Sin and sinners will have been destroyed. What we now see through the eyes of faith will become real. With songs of gladness we enter into the joyful, unrestricted reality of life eternal.

FOUNDATIONS OF FAITH

Closer Look

All scripture is given by inspiration of God. 2 Timothy 3:16.

A wealthy businessman visiting England many years ago saw for the first time a powerful microscope. Looking through its lens, he observed crystals and flower petals, grains of sand, and the intricate design of leaves. Amazed by all the beauty and detail, he decided to purchase a microscope of his own and take it back home with him. There he spent weeks observing the wonders of nature as seen through the remarkable instrument.

One day he examined something he hadn't studied before—food. More precisely, his lunch. Much to his dismay, he discovered tiny living creatures crawling all over his sandwich and strange wiggly things swimming in his soup. Since he was especially fond of the cuisine he was eating, he wasn't quite sure what to do.

Finally he decided that there was only one way to solve his dilemma—he'd destroy the instrument that had uncovered the unsavory fact that his lunch was home to some pretty disgusting-looking life forms. With a vengeance he smashed the microscope to pieces, then enjoyed his food.

The Bible, God's Word, isn't exactly favorite reading among many for the same reason. It becomes a microscope, revealing in vivid detail hidden sins and disgusting habits.

Often those who've discovered the truth about their lives while digging into Scripture simply close the Book and relegate it to the back of the highest shelf in their library. Out of sight. Out of mind.

Mark Twain added another angle when he wrote: "Most people are bothered by those passages of Scripture which they cannot understand; but as for me, I always noticed that the passages in Scripture which trouble me most are those which I do understand."

Like it or not, the Bible has survived basically unchanged for thousands of years. Why? Because it's not just a microscope—it's God's microscope. And the images it reveals about our lives aren't meant to frighten, disgust, or worry us. They seek to motivate us to change what's wrong while we discover what's right. It also provides a detailed look at a life that we should all use as our standard for living—the life of Jesus Christ.

Martin Luther, one of Europe's greatest reformers, told his followers:

"The Bible is alive, it speaks to me.

It has feet, it runs after me.

It has hands, it lays hold of me."

Although one might describe Scripture as simply a collection of words that scribes have carefully, painstakingly copied and translated through the centuries, those words have the power to heal broken hearts, mend shattered spirits, and set wayward feet on the path to heaven. They can change us, motivate us into action, make us better than we are.

So take your time. Gaze long and hard through God's microscope. Although it may reveal the dross of your life, it also offers the powerful cleansing agent of forgiveness with which to wipe it all away.

Divine Egg

*The grace of the Lord Jesus Christ, and the love of God,
and the communion of the Holy Ghost, be with you all. 2 Corinthians 13:14.*

I didn't want to be disturbed. But when he sat down beside me, I knew I was in trouble. His shaven head and collection of beads signaled that the flight was going to be a long one.

Usually I don't mind talking to people. It's interesting to hear about their lives, the challenges they face, the in-depth details of their last medical emergency. But this particular afternoon I just wanted to watch the clouds drift by my 35,000-foot perch and allow my thoughts to wander to things important to me.

To my surprise, however, my companion simply leaned back in his seat, folded his arms over his narrow chest, closed his eyes, and went fast asleep. About an hour later, as I was scanning the articles in one of my church's magazines, I heard a voice beside me. "Do you believe in God?" Apparently my seatmate had awakened from his nap.

"Yes," I responded.

After a long pause he spoke through a yawn. "There are three of Them, you know." His comment was more statement than question.

"That's right," I agreed.

"Kinda like an egg," he continued.

"An egg?"

He straightened himself in his seat and leaned closer to me. "Sure," he said, cupping the fingers of one hand as if cradling something. "See? Here's the outer shell all smooth and round. Then," he cracked open the imaginary object with his other hand, "inside is the white albumen and the yellow yolk. Put them all together and you don't have three things, you have one. An egg! Just like the Godhead. Get it?"

I smiled. "Got it."

With that he refolded his arms with a satisfied sigh and sank back into his seat to continue his nap.

Nice illustration. Here was a guy who was using his head, totally shaven as it may have been, to create a visual representation of a highly complex issue. Although we worship not one but three Beings, yet They are one. Like an egg.

Augustine found himself puzzling over the doctrine of the Trinity one day and decided to go for a walk along the ocean. Soon he discovered a young boy at play, bucket in hand, running back and forth between the breakers and a certain portion of the beach. The Bible scholar watched the lad for a while, then asked him, "Say, young man, what are you doing?"

The lad pointed at an opening in the sand. "I'm trying to put the ocean into this hole," he stated.

Suddenly Augustine realized that he'd been doing the very same thing. He'd been trying to put an infinite God into his finite mind.

The fact that there are three members of the Godhead who work, think, and operate as one might not be conceivable to us. But can we explain how a flower grows or why a heart beats? When we understand, we can believe based on knowledge. But when we don't understand, we need faith. That's the way it is with God—and eggs.

Tasting God

"For God so loved the world that he gave his one and only Son, that whoever believes in him shall not perish but have eternal life." John 3:16, NIV.

To some He's a blessing. To others, a curse. Many call Him "Judge," others, "Father." Just who is God?

A farmer repeatedly invited a friend over to his apple orchard to enjoy the fruit and make some fresh cider. But his acquaintance continually refused. "Thanks, but no thanks," he'd say.

Finally, in frustration, the farmer stated with a sigh, "I guess you're prejudiced against my apples."

"Actually," his friend remarked, "I've tasted a few of them already, and, well, they're very sour."

The farmer's eyebrows rose slightly. "You have? Where exactly were those apples?"

"Along the road over by your fence," came the shy reply. "They'd fallen from the trees and I sampled a few. I knew you wouldn't mind."

"Oh," said the grower, "they are sour, aren't they? But that's as they should be. I placed them there to fool the boys who live nearby. They come to my farm to steal some of my crop. But if you will walk with me to the middle of my orchard, you'll find a very different taste waiting there."

Out on the edges of Christianity some find extremely sour apples: guilt, demands for self-denial, tough guidelines for living a pure, upstanding life. They tend to keep hypocrites and mere dabblers of spirituality at bay. Just briefly tasting the life of commitment and wholesomeness, they find the fruit sour on their tongue.

But in the middle of the orchard, away from the fringes, is where the true seeker of life finds delicious fruit, sweet with promise and overflowing with nourishment. Here, tongues savor the mouthwatering sustenance of life eternal, offered freely by the loving owner of the farm, the Power who watches over all things growing.

The nearer to God, the sweeter the joy.

An elderly man was out walking with his young grandson in a beautiful park. They'd been exploring the trees and bushes, listening to the birds, and reveling in the warm sunshine. At one point the man turned to the child. "How far are you from home?" he asked.

"I don't know, Grandpa," the boy stated.

"Well, *where* are you?"

Again the child answered, "I don't know."

"Sounds to me as if you're lost."

The young boy looked up into the kind eyes of his grandfather. "No. I'm not lost. I'm with you!"

That's the statement God longs to hear fall from our lips when we address Him in prayer. "Lord," we say, "I don't know where I am or where I'm going. But it doesn't matter, because I'm with You."

When this happens, the seeker of truth discovers a new name for God. From that moment on, he simply calls Him "Friend."

Together

"I am the way and the truth and the life.
No one comes to the Father except through me." John 14:6, NIV.

For reasons unknown, you decide to swim from Los Angeles to Hawaii. You hire the finest coaches and train with Olympic gold medal winners. Then you plunge into the Pacific Ocean and head out through the waves, your mind focused on those golden shores many miles away.

After struggling all day and most the night, you realize that you're not going to make it. The ocean is too big, the waves too high, the water too cold. "Help," you call out. "Someone save me!"

Suddenly, through the half-light of dawn, you see a motorboat approaching. "Friend," the captain shouts, "you're in trouble. What you need is the waterproof edition of my latest book, *Swimming to Hawaii*. It'll tell you all you need to know." With a splash the volume lands in the water beside you, and the boat speeds away.

Doesn't sound too helpful? Consider this scenario. The boat pulls up and the captain leans over the railing. "Friend," he shouts, "what you need is someone to show you how to swim. Here, watch me." The captain jumps into the waves next to you. "The secret is the Australian crawl. Watch. See? Breathe, paddle, breathe, paddle. Just follow my example, and you'll make it." With that the instructor climbs back into his boat and hurries away.

Still doesn't seem that helpful? Perhaps this would be more to your liking. The motorboat pulls up alongside you and strong arms lift you onto the deck. "Friend," says the captain, "let me save you. Here, have some cookies and milk. They'll give you energy. There, don't you feel better already? Great. Now, back into the water you go. Hawaii is only 1,000 miles away. Good luck!"

Allow just one more possibility. You're dying in the water, your strength and will exhausted. "Save me," you gasp. "Someone save me."

From the mists approaches a motorboat. The captain shouts, "Hold on; I'm coming." Then he leaps into the water, wraps strong arms around you, and pulls you to the safety of the boat. He feeds you, places blankets about your shoulders, and sits by your side as the fear and terror of the night dissipate in the morning light.

Then, after he knows you're out of danger, he turns the boat toward Hawaii and, with you safely in his care, churns through the waves. At long last he ties his vessel up at the dock in Waikiki. Carrying you gently down the ramp, he places you on golden sands. "We did it," he says. "We did it together."

The service Jesus offers the world goes far beyond what's written in any book. It's more than a how-to set of instructions or a nourishing meal filled with promises and hope. In Jesus we find true salvation. His presence brings us much more than education and sustenance. Lifting our burdens and carrying them on His back, He allows us to continue our journey supported by His love, forgiveness, and presence.

And on that glorious day when we stand beside Him in heaven facing the smiling countenance of our heavenly Father, Jesus will look into our eyes and proudly say, *"We did it. We did it together."*

Filling Up

And I will pray the Father, and he shall give you
another Comforter, that he may abide with you for ever. John 14:16.

A founder of Gordon Conwell Divinity School, A. J. Gordon, was out for a walk when he saw a peculiar sight. A house stood across a field near a grove of trees. Beside the house was what looked like a man pumping furiously above a wellhead. As Gordon watched, the man moved the handle up and down, up and down continuously, tirelessly, without slowing or taking a rest.

After it had gone on for some time, the preacher decided he just had to find out how that man could work so hard for so long without stopping. He headed across the field in the direction of the house. As he got closer, he suddenly realized that the individual at the well wasn't an actual person, but a wooden figure painted and shaped to look like a man. The arm that pumped so rapidly was hinged at the elbow. The hand was wired to the handle. The water poured from the faucet not because the figure was working so hard, but because of the action of an artesian well hidden below the surface of the ground. In reality, the water was pumping the man!

Scripture calls the Holy Spirit many things: Comforter, Counselor, Companion,

Teacher, and even Wind. He works unseen. But the results of His labors are obvious.

You may ask, "How do I know that the Holy Spirit is living in me?" The same way you know there's music on a cassette tape, images on the film hidden in your camera, or that an airplane will fly. In complete confidence, you listen to the tape, enjoy the pictures after they've been developed, and hurry to a loved one's side using the services of the local airline. We may not know how or why; we just know that things happen. That's the way it is when the Holy Spirit fills a life.

Christian writer Roy Hession, in his book *Be Filled Now,* offers a beautiful illustration. "To be filled with the Holy Spirit is to be filled with one who is already there, in our hearts. Take up a sponge and while it is in your hand squeeze it. In that condition, plunge it in water and submerge it, keeping it there. It is now in the water and the water is in it. As you hold it in the water, you open your hand, and as you do so the water fills all the pores which you release in this way. It is now filled with the water. When we receive Christ we are born anew and put into that sphere where the Holy Spirit is operating and the Holy Spirit comes to reside in us."

However, filling is only part of the picture. To expand on Hession's imagery, we can also conclude that a sponge is much more useful wet than dry. It's the combination of the sponge and the water that makes it possible to wash, scrub, or purify.

"What God chooses, He cleanses.

What God cleanses, He molds.

What God molds, He fills.

What God fills, He uses."

—J. S. Baxter

The prayer of every Christian should be "Fill me, O God!"

Chance

In the beginning God created the heaven and the earth. Genesis 1:1.

A much admired science professor constructed a precisely scaled model of the solar system. He worked on it for months, preparing every detail, measuring every angle, computing every orbit. When he had it completed, it was a masterpiece of science and technology.

One day a student came to the professor's office almost breathless with wonder. "That model!" he gasped. "It's amazing! I've never seen such beauty and precision. Who made it?"

The instructor shrugged. "No one."

"No one?" the student blinked. "Come on, professor. You can tell me. Who made that exquisite creation?"

"No one," the educator repeated. "It just happened. I walked into my lab one day and there it was."

The student became confused and angry. "How can you say that?" he demanded. "Something as awesome as that doesn't just happen!"

Even before the words had finished leaving the visitor's lips, the professor answered,

"Young man, if you can go out of my science classroom and look around at nature and believe that all of the wonders of the world just happened, you must believe that *this* precise piece of work suddenly appeared without a creator as well."

To enjoy any degree of hope for the future, we must reach a fundamental conclusion to the question Did we just happen? Or did a creator set in motion the life forces that pump our hearts and spark our thoughts? Unless we address the question fully, faith becomes an exercise in futility.

Someone once asked artist Salvador Dali, "Is it hard to paint a picture?"

He shook his head. "No. It's either easy or impossible."

It's the same with the creation of the universe. For God, it was easy. For every other power, including human, it's impossible. If we believe that the marvels of science and nature are the result of a mysterious cosmic game of chance played out over eons of time, we're negating our only hope for eternal life, because the same God who spoke our world into existence will someday create our future home in heaven. Without God there would be no world. And without God, there will be no world to come.

Robert Jastrow, a scientist who considers himself an agnostic when it comes to religious matters, once wrote: "A sound explanation may exist for the explosive birth of our universe, but if it does, science cannot find out what that explanation is. The scientist's pursuit of the past ends in the moment of creation. This is an exceedingly strange development. For the scientist who has lived by his faith in the power of reason, the story ends like a bad dream. He has scaled the mountains of ignorance; he is about to conquer the highest peak; as he pulls himself over the final rock, he is greeted by a band of theologians who have been sitting there for centuries" *(God and the Astronomers* [New York: Norton, 1978]).

The humanistic view of science begins in the unknown and ends at death. The Christian view of science awakens at the dawn of Creation and endures forever.

Image Is Everything

*Then God said, "Let us make man
in our image, in our likeness." Genesis 1:26, NIV.*

The other day I was doing some landscaping in my yard when I happened to glance down at my soil-stained fingers. My breath caught in my throat when I realized that the hands that occupied the ends of my arms weren't mine. They were my father's.

I sat studying them for a long moment. The narrow fingers, thick palms, exposed veins, bumpy knuckles—all were exact replicas of my dad's hardworking hands. A feeling of pride swept over me, pride in the fact that I shared so much with the gentle man who, along with my beautiful mother, had given me life.

Even as I sat there surrounded by turned soil and blowing leaves, a deeper thought surfaced in my mind. How much of me reflects the God who breathed life into my first ancestor Adam, a man who forms the root of every family tree?

It's not enough for me to tell the world that I'm a product of the Creator's power. Nor is it enough to recite His words or study His laws of love. I want every part of me to reflect His image. I long for people to see Him when they look at me. But how can I do that? So much time and sin separates us all from the hand that formed our noble ancestor.

A child stands gazing at a freshly opened box of chocolate candies. His lips press together in thought as his brow furrows slightly. "Only one, and no more," his mother instructs. Should it be the biggest piece? Or would the small round one be his favorite—peppermint cream? Of course, the long one in the corner would last longer.

Which to choose? How to decide?

Little does he know it, but that boy is experiencing the greatest gift the Creator has bestowed upon humanity. It's what sets him apart from all of nature, from all the beasts of the fields or birds of the air. He's being forced to make a decision because God designed his mind to utilize the most incredible power in the universe—choice. No other earthly creature fully has it.

Nature generally operates by instinct. Birds migrate, fish swim, lions hunt, and flowers bloom because of it. But humanity functions at a completely different level of consciousness. We do what we do as a direct result of choices, personal or collective. It's what we share with each other—and with God.

Here is where I find the answer to my question. If I desire to echo God's love to a hurting world, then His choices must become my choices. The way I choose to love must reflect His love. His hands must work through mine, His words fall from my lips, His feet guide my feet as I travel the spiritual path to heaven.

Someday, our faces and our bodies will once again reflect the image of God. Our connection to the Creator will be evident even in the way we smile. But until then, we can announce to the world that we're children of the heavenly King by daily demonstrating our heritage through the choices we make.

A Note Out of Tune

And there was war in heaven. Revelation 12:7.

A man stopped by the music studio of an old friend. By way of greeting he said with a smile, "Professor, what's the good news today?"

The old teacher silently stood, walked across the room, picked up a small hammer, and struck a tuning fork. As the single note reverberated throughout the chamber, the musician said, "That's A. It's A today, it was A 5,000 years ago, and it will be A 1,000 years from now. The soprano upstairs sings off-key, the tenor across the hall flats his high notes, and the piano downstairs is in desperate need of tuning." He struck the fork again. "But no matter what anyone thinks, no matter what anyone does, this is still A. And that's the good news for today."

A long time ago the universe heard, for the first time, a note out of tune. Its dissonance echoed from star to star, system to system, planet to planet. Ears used to hearing the perfect harmonies of heaven found the note disturbing, troubling, frightening. Someone was singing off-key. Someone's praise was falling a little flat. Someone needed tuning.

According to Scripture, that someone was Lucifer, the covering cherub. "You were the model of perfection," Ezekiel laments in Ezekiel 28:12. "You were . . . full of wisdom and perfect in beauty. . . . You were blameless in your ways from the day you were created till wickedness was found in you" (verses 12-15, NIV).

How such an unsettling event could happen in God's universe remains shrouded in divine mystery. But this much we know. Our earth became the center of discord.

"You won't die," Satan told Eve in the garden as he tempted her into rejecting God's command to stay away from forbidden fruit. "God's not telling the truth. I am." And from that moment on a great conflict raged on our world, a battle not only between good and evil, but between truth and lies.

For some today, it has come to the point where the line separating truth from error appears blurred. No longer are the boundaries clearly marked. The New Age movement clearly illustrates this. In four basic tenets this dangerous philosophy demonstrates that the battle between God and Satan is far from over.

According to those who follow its teachings, death does not exist, only regeneration or the movement from one conscious level to another. Yet the voice of God still proclaims that "the wages of sin is death" (Romans 6:23).

"You are divine," New Agers insist. "You can be your own god." "No one comes to the Father except through me," Jesus states in John 14:6 (NIV).

"Sin is only a state of mind. It doesn't exist," proponents of the movement announce. "All have sinned, and come short of the glory of God," says Jesus through Paul in Romans 3:23.

"Since there is no sin, there's no judgment," soothe the New Agers. The apostle Paul paints a very different picture. Near the end of his life he wrote, "I have fought the good fight, I have finished the race, I have kept the faith. Now there is in store for me the crown of righteousness, which the Lord, the righteous Judge, will award to me on that day—and not only to me, but also to all who have longed for his appearing" (2 Timothy 4:7, 8, NIV).

Who's telling the truth? God? Satan? Every human being who walks the dusty paths of our world must decide which is true and which isn't. In spite of what note others may sing, there has always been and always will be only one A.

Sacrifice

"Is it nothing to you, all you who pass by?" Lamentations 1:12, NIV.

During the Great Depression a Missouri man named John Griffith operated a railroad drawbridge spanning the mighty Mississippi River. On a warm summer day in 1937 he took his 8-year-old son, Greg, to work with him, proudly showing the lad how he raised the bridge to allow boats to pass underneath, then lowered it again whenever trains approached.

At noon John put the bridge up so boats could sail through and settled himself on the observation deck with his son. Minutes slipped by unnoticed as the two enjoyed their lunch. Suddenly the shrieking of a train whistle in the distance startled the man. Glancing at his watch, he saw that it was 1:07. The Memphis Express with 400 passengers on board was roaring toward the raised bridge! Jumping to his feet, he ran back to the control tower and prepared to lower the trestle.

Just before throwing the master lever, he looked down to make sure all boats were safely out of the way. That's when he saw, to his horror, that Greg had slipped from the observation deck and become caught in the massive gears that controlled the bridge. Desperately John's mind whirled, trying to come up with a rescue plan, but there was no way to save his son as well as the lives of those on board the train. With alarming closeness, the whistle shrieked again. He could hear the clattering of the wheels as 400 people rushed toward the bridge where his son lay caught in the gears.

John knew what he had to do. Burying his head in his left arm, he pushed the master switch forward. The massive trestle lowered into place just as the Memphis Express swept into view and roared across the river.

When the operator lifted his head, he stared at the passing train through agonizing tears. Through the open windows he saw businessmen casually reading their afternoon papers, fashionably dressed women sipping coffee in the dining car, and children digging long spoons into tall dishes of ice cream. No one noticed the control house. No one glanced at the great gearbox. With breaking heart and soul-wrenching sobs, John Griffith cried out at the passing train, "I sacrificed my son for you people! Don't you care? Don't you even care?"

Today, we can hear a Father's voice above the tumult of our lives. As we hurry along, lost in the challenges we all face, the heartbreaking question rings down through the centuries. "Charles . . . Helen . . . Tasha . . . Nathan . . . Tristan . . . I sacrificed My Son for you. Don't you care? Don't you care?"

Christ died because there was no other way to save humanity. As the Father of love looked down from heaven's portals, the obedient Son closed His eyes and fell under the temporary spell of sin, ending the most perfect life our world will ever know. But, praise God, that same death set in motion a series of events that will culminate with our glorious reunion with the Saviour who sacrificed Himself for our sins.

Yes, Father, we care. We care very much.

Unshaven

He has given us his very great and precious promises, so that through them
you may participate in the divine nature and escape
the corruption in the world caused by evil desires. 2 Peter 1:4, NIV.

A popular barber rode through the slums of a large city with a favorite customer, a minister. The two had had many discussions about religion, but nothing the pastor said seemed to move his friend out of his lethargy concerning things eternal.

As they drove along, the barber shook his head and pointed out the window. "If there's a loving God," he said, "how can He permit such poverty, suffering, and violence among these people? Why doesn't He just save them from all this trouble?"

About that time a disheveled, raggedly dressed bum crossed the street, swaying back and forth, his long, scraggly hair hanging matted about his neck, his chin covered with a month's growth of beard. Turning to his companion, the minister motioned in the direction of the pedestrian. "Say, you're a barber and claim to be a good one. So why do you allow that man over there to appear so unkempt and unshaven?"

"Why, why," the barber stuttered, "that fellow never gave me a chance to fix him up. Not once has his shadow ever darkened my doorstep. I could transform him into a new man, but he won't let me."

"Exactly," the minister said. "Most of the time men and women experience what they go through because they reject God's help."

I once sat in church listening to my father-in-law, Pastor Harold Kuebler, preach a Sabbath sermon. One of the illustrations he presented struck home to my heart in a profound way. He told his congregation that he'd been driving his car for several years and had always had a hard time starting it, especially in cold weather. "The starter just grinds away, but the engine refuses to catch," he explained.

Then he told us that one day he was rummaging through the glove compartment when he happened upon the automobile's operator's manual. Leafing through untouched pages of the book, he noticed a whole section dedicated to starting the car in cold and in hot weather. It didn't take him long to discover that he'd been doing it all wrong, flooding the engine, causing excessive wear and tear on the poor starter, and wasting gas in the process. From that moment on, cold morning start-ups were easy. All he had to do was follow the instructions that had been available to him all along.

Salvation requires two things of us: acceptance and obedience. They're both necessary, both part of our journey to heaven.

First, we accept the help God freely offers. He takes our unshaven, matted spiritual lives and transforms us by His power. Then He outlines a plan of action built around His laws of love, detailing just how we can best maintain our walk with Him. God shows us how to operate our lives to their fullest potentials no matter how hot or cold the winds of strife may blow.

However, if we reject His help, if we ignore His Word and choose to walk the streets alone, we leave ourselves wide open to Satan's devastating attacks.

Need a trim? Feeling a little unshaven lately? Has it been a while since you browsed through your Bible looking for answers? God waits. God loves. God saves.

Members

Let us not give up meeting together, as some are in the habit of doing,
but let us encourage one another—and all the more
as you see the Day approaching. Hebrews 10:25, NIV.

The pastor of a church noticed that a certain parishioner who'd been quite regular in attending weekly services suddenly stopped coming. After a few weeks had passed, the minister decided it was time to visit the absent member.

One chilly evening he knocked on the door of the man's home and found him alone, seated before a blazing fire. The member welcomed him in and led him to a big chair by the hearth. The parishioner figured he knew why the visitor had come and waited to hear a lecture on church faithfulness.

Instead the two sat in silence, saying nothing. Together they contemplated the flickering flames of the fire, feeling its warmth and enjoying the deep aroma of burning wood. At long last the minister rose and walked over to the hearth. He took the fire tongs hanging nearby and carefully plucked a brightly burning ember from the flames and placed it to one side, away from the logs. Then he sat back down in his chair and remained silent. The host watched in quiet fascination.

As more minutes ticked by, they both noticed that the lowly ember began to lose its brilliant glow. Slowly it darkened, until finally it stopped producing any heat whatsoever. It had become a charred and useless chunk of ash.

No one had said a word since the initial greeting. But as the minister rose to leave, the parishioner took his hand in his. "Thank you, Pastor," he said quietly. "Thank you for your visit, and especially for your fiery sermon. I'll be at church next week."

When God created the concept of church, He designed it to be far more than a place where believers gather together and discuss religion. He meant for it to be an open hearth where shared praise could warm lives. God wanted to create a fire in souls, to prepare a place where the flames of spiritual passion could be fed through collective service for others. And just as important, God desired that shared communion would energize individual lives.

Oliver Cromwell, ruler of England in the mid-1600s, when faced with a shortage of precious metal for coins, sent his troops out into the country to find some. They returned with the report that the only precious metals they could locate had been used for statues of saints standing in the corners of churches.

"Fine," Cromwell said. "Melt down the saints and put them in circulation immediately."

It is a beautiful illustration of what God has in mind for His church. "Melt the hearts of My people," He says to every pastor and lay worker throughout His kingdom of love, "and put them in circulation."

Some best hear echoes of God's love within the warmth of shared worship, amid the fiery passion of service, or while sitting comfortably beside other saints on a Sabbath morning.

Transformation

And we, who with unveiled faces all reflect the Lord's glory,
are being transformed into his likeness
with ever-increasing glory. 2 Corinthians 3:18, NIV.

We'd ridden for hours along the dusty road. Every few minutes a truck burdened with freshly cut logs would speed by in the opposite direction, throwing thick clouds of red-colored dust over us, filling our nostrils, stinging our eyes, making breathing difficult.

I checked to make sure that my equipment was still protected from the swirling grime. If I was to return with a photographic record of what we saw, I had to protect at all cost the cameras and film hidden within the cases at my feet.

My assignment was simple. Travel into the South American jungle and take motion pictures of a certain village filled with unique people. What made them unique? Every member of the settlement was a Christian. Unlike their neighbors who worshiped many gods, some of whom they said lived in trees and rivers and snakes, these men, women, and children worshiped only one: the God of heaven.

The villages we passed revealed in vivid detail the poverty that gripped the land. Far from the relative wealth of the cities, these villagers spent their days doing little more than trying to survive. Because of their great need, they had little self-esteem. Their houses, yards, and roadways reflected the emptiness and discouragement filling their hearts. The surroundings were unsanitary, to say the least.

Our much-traveled vehicle slowed, turned off the main road, and headed deeper into the jungle. After more time and miles had passed, we came upon a small isolated village set in a clearing beside the rushing rapids of a river. The driver found a shaded spot under a grove of trees and turned off the ignition.

Looking at the world through the viewfinder of a camera offers a highly focused perspective. As film moved silently behind my lens, I witnessed the daily lives of a people whose very existence had been transformed. Their simple houses, furnished with only the bare essentials, were clean and orderly. The lawns were clipped, the roads well marked and potholes filled. Where were the wandering pigs, the piles of refuse, the unmistakable odors of disease? What about the ragged-looking children and the ashen faces of their parents? These people looked healthy and lean, eyes clear, faces shining with hope. Had this village really once been like the others? Was such an amazing change possible?

Someone led me to the small log-and-thatch house of the missionary teacher for the area. He welcomed me with a broad smile and allowed me the privilege of seeing the place he called home. Through the eye of my camera I observed a grass mat on the floor, a neatly folded blanket, a tiny dresser sitting low by the bed, and a pair of sandals.

Then I understood. Resting on the blanket was the cause for the transformation, the reason this village looked, smelled, and sounded so different from all the rest. With its covers worn from use and pages yellowed by time, a copy of God's Word waited in the stillness of the stifling afternoon air, ready to lift the spirit of reader and hearer alike, ready to create clear images of how life is supposed to be lived even when burdened with poverty. The owner of that Bible had taken the words to heart and was spreading the good news throughout the village.

That was his mission. It should be ours as well.

Unity

Now the body is not made up of
one part but of many. 1 Corinthians 12:14, NIV.

A visitor to a mental institution noticed what seemed to be a potentially hazardous situation. He observed three guards watching more than 100 dangerous inmates. "Aren't you afraid that these people will overpower the guards and escape?" he asked.

"Oh, no," his guide assured him. "There's no danger of that happening."

"Why?" the visitor wanted to know.

"Simple. The mentally ill never unite."

In our day of independent thinking, of finding one's "inner self," of creating one's own way in the world, something has been lost. Church administrators have discovered that many who occupy their pews on Sabbath morning have a somewhat different view of life than their parents or grandparents. They seem to be saying, "Hey, Church, what do you have to offer me today? I'm a busy person and don't have time for mind games or theological mumbo jumbo. Just tell me how to live and let me get back to what I think is important as quickly and effortlessly as possible."

In times past, ranchers and farmers who didn't want their horses frightened or distracted by what happened around them placed blinders over the animals' eyes, narrowing their field of view. The horses could see only what was straight ahead of them.

Is the same thing happening in your church today? Are some Christians allowing the devil to place social blinders over their eyes, narrowing their field of view until they see only their own needs and desires? If that's the case, it's cause for alarm and sadness. God's ideal for His church isn't independence, but rather *de*pendence.

Some years ago two students graduated from Chicago's Kent College of Law. Overton was the highest-ranking scholar in his class. When he stood to receive his diploma, he insisted that half the credit for his success should go to his friend Kaspryzak. The two first met at the top of a long flight of stairs. Overton, who was blind, heard a voice beside him. "Here, let me help you." It was Kaspryzak, a man who had no arms. Together they descended the stairs.

The chance meeting soon ripened into a long-lasting friendship and a beautiful example of interdependence. The blind student carried the books for the armless man who read aloud during study sessions. For years the strengths of one compensated the deficiency of the other.

A little child in an African tribe wandered off into tall jungle grass by his village and became lost. Family and friends searched all day, but failed to find him. The next morning members of the tribe came up with a plan. They'd all hold hands and walk through the grass together. Sure enough, they found the missing child, but the cold night had been too much for him, and he had died of exposure. In anguish the mother cried out, "Oh, if only we had held hands sooner."

It's time for those of us who profess to be Christians to throw off our blinders. We need to combine our strengths and, taking the hand of the person sitting in the pew next to us, move out together to search for the lost. In doing so, we may also assure our own salvation.

Buried Alive!

*We were therefore buried with him through baptism into death
in order that, just as Christ was raised from the dead
through the glory of the Father, we too may live a new life. Romans 6:4, NIV.*

The car ground to a halt, and we spilled out, lugging cameras, tripods, film boxes, and extra batteries. High overhead, the sun hung hot in a hazy, humid sky. "Get lots of close-ups," the project director admonished as we made our way along a dusty path winding through a stand of trees. "I want to see the smiles when they come up."

I'd photographed baptisms before. This one, which happened to be taking place in Central America, I believed wouldn't be a lot different. The minister would say his little speech, the candidate would be lowered under the water, and that's it. *Click, click,* done.

As we emerged from the jungle we found ourselves on the bank of a wide river. To our right waited a surprisingly large gathering of people arranged in colorful groups, their faces flushed with excitement. I estimated more than 3,000 in attendance. Where'd they come from? I thought we were in the middle of nowhere, miles from any town.

"Most of them left their houses before dawn and walked here," the director said, answering my unspoken question.

"Walked? In this heat?"

My companion smiled. "Baptism is a big thing in this country," he stated. "That's probably why we have so many of them."

Nodding, I started looking for a good vantage point from which to take my pictures. I figured if all these people had worked so hard to get here on this steamy Sabbath afternoon, the least I could do was get some great photographs of the proceedings.

"How many are being baptized?" I asked almost as an afterthought.

"Oh," the director wiped sweat from his brow, "I think between 600 and 700."

"Hundred?" I paused in my work.

"That's a relatively small number compared to some services I've attended," he replied.

Before long a man whom I was told was the principal evangelist in the area waded out into the water and presented a short sermon. I didn't understand what he was saying, but the people on the bank sure did. They listened with silent, breathless concentration, drinking in every word. Then he lifted his hands over his head and motioned for something to happen. Immediately two dozen more pastors waded out into the river, taking up positions about 15 feet apart from each other and forming a long line not far from shore. Then queues of people—young, old, male, female, rich, and poor—snaked from the bank and out into the water. With a prayer and a song, the baptisms began.

I moved through the crowds, splashing out into the river, hurrying from one smiling pastor to the next, zooming in on the wet, joyous faces of the various individuals as they rose from their liquid graves.

An onlooker's boat floated nearby, and I asked (with waving arms and friendly grins) if he'd take me farther out into the river so I could photograph back toward the shore. The man at the oars quickly agreed, and we made our way across the waves. Switching to my telephoto lens, I got great images of pastors and their candidates framed against the colorful backdrop of proud, loving faces.

Sitting there under the stifling sun, watching people being lowered, two dozen at a time, into a muddy river, the true meaning of baptism suddenly struck me. In a land in which rituals and dangerous misconceptions about God held so many lives captive, these people had chosen truth over tradition. Each of them had walked miles to demonstrate publicly, by allowing themselves to be lowered into a polluted river, that they'd found spiritual truth. They were altering their lives, bucking the system, making a stand for what they believed.

My camera captured more than a baptismal service that day. It recorded with light and shadows and color a major shift of priorities in the hearts of almost 700 people. Their lives would be forever changed because, on a hot Sabbath afternoon, they'd died to the past and rose to begin a new life in Christ.

Broken Flesh

Take, eat; this is my body. Matthew 26:26.

It contains the remains of more than 244,000 veterans, their dependents, and many political leaders. Most of those from the armed forces died in battle. At one time the site was part of a garden.

Arlington National Cemetery, across the Potomac River from Washington, D.C., sits on a hillside below an aging mansion. In years past Confederate general Robert E. Lee and his wife, Mary, had walked among the flowers growing there, reveling in the warmth of spring air or seeking shade under the large trees lining the property. Then, in 1864, while our nation staggered under the weight of a horrific civil war, Union forces confiscated the mansion and grounds and transformed them into a cemetery for Union dead. Years after the war, the U.S. Supreme Court ruled that the property rightfully belonged to Lee's son George, and the government paid him handsomely for it.

Visitors who stroll through the seemingly endless rows of white crosses, most marking the final resting places of national heroes, do so in hushed tones. One thought remains focused in their minds. A vast majority of these people gave their lives so future generations could live in freedom and unity.

One night long ago Christ gathered His disciples about Him in an upper room and prepared to enjoy a meal. Servants had placed bread on the low table in front of them and poured fresh grape juice. Plates rested by the elbow of each member of the dinner party. Conversation turned to the reason for the meal—the Passover feast, a once-a-year celebration familiar to all Jews. Their ancestors had once prepared a hurried meal, and when it was finished, they'd turned their backs on Egyptian bondage and begun a journey that eventually led them to the Promised Land.

At that moment Jesus did and said something totally unexpected. He reached out and took hold of a circle of bread, offered thanks for it, and began ripping it apart into smaller sections. Then, to the astonishment of the disciples, He said, "This is My body. Eat it."

It wasn't in the ritual, wasn't part of a normal Passover meal. What was Jesus thinking? Then the Saviour poured the grape juice into their cups while proclaiming, "This is My blood. Drink it."

Wait a minute! What's going on? It was supposed to be a meal celebrating a nation's separation from cruel bondage, and here was the Master sounding disgustingly like a cannibal. The disciples probably looked at each other, then shrugged and shook their heads. Their Leader was always coming up with strange parables for them to ponder. Here was probably just another puzzle with a deeper meaning hidden somewhere. They'd think about it later. Now they were hungry.

The next day the meaning of the puzzle revealed itself in terrifying detail as Jesus died, His body broken, His blood spilled.

On a hillside overlooking Washington, D.C., stand acres of crosses marking the places where heroes lay buried. On a hillside overlooking Jerusalem, a single cross lifted the Son of God above the earth and gave future heroes something for which to die.

Fitness for Service

It was he who gave some to be apostles, some to be prophets, some to be evangelists, and some to be pastors and teachers. Ephesians 4:11, NIV.

A schoolboy was trying out for a play. His mother, seeing how set he was on getting a part, feared that he might not be chosen and that the decision would crush him emotionally. She arrived at the school on the day the director awarded the parts. The boy rushed up to her, eyes shining with pride and excitement. "Mommy, Mommy," he shouted breathlessly. "Guess what?"

"What?" the mother asked as she hugged her son.

The young child smiled broadly. "I've been chosen to clap and cheer!"

God bestows upon members of His church an endless stream of spiritual gifts. According to the apostle Paul such gifts may include abilities and talents, mental strengths, spiritual insights, and even the rare capability of peering into the future. Paul suggests in 1 Corinthians 12:31 that we should desire the "best gifts," which means we should strive to develop and perfect them in our lives.

As wonderful and desirable as spiritual gifts may be, there might be more to them than meets the eye.

On a snowy morning at 5:00 a.m., a candidate for missionary service rang the bell at the home of the church leader who assigned and coordinated overseas appointments. A servant ushered the visitor into the parlor, where he sat for three hours beyond the time scheduled for his interview. At long last the administrator appeared and began his questioning.

"Can you spell?" the officer of the church asked.

Somewhat mystified, the candidate nodded. "Yes, sir."

"Fine. Spell 'baker.'"

"B-A-K-E-R."

The examiner made a mark in his notebook. "Do you know anything about numbers?"

"Yes. A bit."

"Good. Please add 2 plus 2."

"Four."

"Great." The questioner stood to his feet. "I believe you have passed. I'll inform the church board tomorrow. You'll be hearing from us soon."

At the board meeting the administrator gave his report of the interview. He said, "The candidate has all the qualifications of a fine missionary. First, I tested him on self-denial, making him arrive at my home at 5:00 a.m. Second, I tested him on promptness. He rang the bell exactly on the hour. Third, I examined him for patience by making him wait for three hours to see me. Fourth, I tested him on temper. He showed no anger or aggravation. Fifth, I tried his humility by asking him questions any 7-year-old could answer, but he showed no resentment. Yes, I believe the candidate meets the requirements."

It's my opinion that when God bestows spiritual gifts on His people, He's accomplishing far more than providing a way to spread the good news of salvation throughout the world. He's also creating an avenue by which He can obtain a clear indication of our fitness for service and our willingness to use whatever gift we possess to glorify His name. God wants more than our hands and feet—He wants our hearts and minds as well.

Cows' Tails

"In the last days, God says, I will pour out my Spirit on all people.
Your sons and daughters will prophesy, your young men will
see visions, your old men will dream dreams." Acts 2:17, NIV.

It's like walking through a circus: "Three-headed Dog-Man Discovered in Suburban Basement." "Secret Occult Meetings Held at the White House." "Lost Gospels of Christ Reveal Astonishing Prophecies." "Astrologers Predict Destruction of West Coast Cities." Headlines from a dozen tabloid magazines scream at us as we wait to purchase our groceries.

Why all this focus on the bizarre, incredible, and mysterious? The answer is simple. Besides enjoying a good scare, people long to know the future. They want to know how to plan so that tomorrow or the next day won't take them by surprise. That way they can be prepared for whatever comes, whether it's good or bad.

Can't say as I blame them. A few days of my own past I'd like to live over again with a little more preparation.

God knew that about us, so He made some astonishing arrangements. He gave the gift of prophecy to a long list of individuals throughout history, showing them in vivid detail or through symbolic images what was to come. Isaiah, Jeremiah, Ezekiel, Daniel, and John the revelator all peered into the future and saw both wonderful and horrifying events.

The Chinese have a most interesting saying. In words pregnant with meaning, they insist that "it's very difficult to prophesy, especially about the future."

Dr. Charles C. Ryrie pointed out that, using the law of chance, it would require 200 billion earths populated with 4 billion people each to come up with one person who could achieve 100 accurate prophecies without errors in sequence. Yet the Bible records numerous prophecies fulfilled to the letter at Christ's *first* coming! Can we trust the predictions concerning His second?

What's the secret of Scripture's success?

We're all prophets of sorts. For example, we know that if we wander outside in a snowstorm without a coat, we *will* get cold. If we stop eating and drinking, we *will* die. However, we're limited because we can't see beyond our own reality. But God can. He can move through time with the same ease that we walk from room to room in our house. So if God says something is going to happen, I believe Him not only because He can see into the future, but because He can experience the future firsthand.

Here's a simple test by which to determine if you should believe those headlines shouting from the checkout counter. First, does the message agree with the Bible? After all, Scripture is our only shining example of prophetic accuracy. Second, do the predictions come true? Strange how those magazines seem to ignore their failure rates and just concentrate on new predictions each year. Three, do they recognize Christ? Remember, He's the only Being who can actually experience the future firsthand. Fourth, what about the prophet? Is the person making his or her prediction living a life in harmony with the God who knows the future? If not, any predictions will only be, at best, educated guesses.

Once as he was trying to make a point, Abraham Lincoln realized that the person he was talking to was being stubborn. So the president tried a different tack. "How many legs does a cow have?" he asked.

"Four, of course," came the disgusted reply.

"That's right," Lincoln said with a nod. "Now, suppose you call the cow's tail a leg. How many legs would the cow then have?"

The opponent thought for a minute. "Why, five."

The president leaned forward in his chair. "That's where you're wrong, my friend," he said softly. "Calling a cow's tail a leg doesn't make it a leg."

Calling a prophecy a prophecy doesn't make it so. Only when the prediction agrees with Scripture, recognizes Christ's authority, and comes through someone whose life reflects that authority can it be trusted. All other predictions are but cows' tails.

Chocolate-covered Sin

I would not have known what sin was
except through the law. Romans 7:7, NIV.

Medical science has discovered that some individuals are physiologically sensitive to chocolate. While I can't imagine such a terrible condition, it's true. Their bodies react, sometimes violently, to the larger doses of benzene compounds found in chocolate. Depending on the level of sensitivity, reactions can range from mild, producing minor skin rashes, to very severe, resulting in physiological shock and even death.

Chocolate is fatal to some people not because it's poisonous in and of itself, but because of the biochemical makeup of their bodies. In other words, chocolate isn't what kills. Their *reaction* to the chocolate ends their life.

God's law operates under the same principle. He designed it to produce an adverse reaction in our lives whenever sin enters. No sin. No adverse reaction. Yet for centuries people have blamed God's laws for their ills. "God is punishing me," they lament. "He's making me suffer because of the bad things I've done."

A man who lived in an extremely oppressive culture moved to the United States. In his country it was illegal to walk on the sidewalks after 6:00 p.m. Soon after arriving in

America he decided to see the sights of his new surroundings and went for a stroll into town. Suddenly he realized that it was very close to 6:00 p.m. and began running back toward his neighborhood. He soon saw that he wasn't going to make it in time.

"Please, sir," he called to the driver of a passing automobile, "I'm far from my house and it's almost 6:00. If I continue walking on the sidewalk I'll be arrested. Can you give me a ride?"

The motorist frowned, trying to figure out why the man was so agitated and frightened. Then he realized that the person must be new to the United States. "Let me assure you, friend, that here in this country we do not arrest people for being out after 6:00," he said with a smile. "Keep walking. You're breaking no laws here."

Even though living in a land built on individual freedom, the new arrival was trying to be obedient to the laws he'd left behind. They were still controlling him. As yet, he had not placed in his heart and mind the laws of the new land where freedom reigned. Same sidewalk, same 6:00 hour, different reaction based on which law fills the heart.

It's the responsibility of all Christians to reject the laws of Satan that advocate such fearful temperaments as selfishness, greed, and personal supremacy, and instead become familiar with the laws of God. We are to study them, examine them under the microscope of reality, and fit them securely into our hearts. Then any adverse reactions we may experience will simply be a clear indicator that some type of evil has tried to make inroads into our thoughts and actions. When the devil attempts to reach us, we're repelled by his presence, horrified by his suggestions, angered by his insistence. "The sacred law written in my heart is reacting against you," we shout. "You're making me spiritually ill. Go away. *Go away!*"

Then we nestle ourselves in the arms of Jesus and enjoy the sweetness of His love.

Changing Focus

And God blessed the seventh day and made it holy, because on it
he rested from all the work of creating that he had done. Genesis 2:3, NIV.

Don't talk to a preacher about Sabbath rest. It's typically his or her busiest day! However, even within the tumult of such responsibility God's people can still enjoy that blessed rest because Sabbath isn't a time to stop working, it's a time to change focus.

Professional cameras boast a vital piece of hardware. Surrounding the lens you'll find a focusing ring carefully engraved so fingers can grip it easily. When you turn the ring while gazing through the viewfinder, you'll notice something amazing. Portions of the scene you're attempting to photograph will drift in and out of focus, becoming blurry, then sharp, and then blurry again.

Photographers use the phenomenon to selectively focus on what's most important in the scene. If they're trying to capture the smile of a child standing near the camera, they'll focus on the face and allow the background to become a blur. But if it's the distant mountain they want to capture, what's near the camera isn't important so they'll allow those portions of the scene to become undistinguishable.

Such "selective focusing" can also get you out of trouble—a fact I discovered one day in Beirut, Lebanon. I was taking pictures at the city's international airport for my church paper. A Christian missionary pilot was ferrying a small airplane from the United States to Korea and had landed at the airport for some rest and fuel. My editor wanted to write about his visit.

A few days before the pilot's arrival, Beirut International Airport had been the target of a military attack from a nation to the south. Air raids had blown up a number of empty passenger airliners—this latest carnage part of an ongoing struggle between nations that began in Abraham's time. The burnt, skeletal remains of the airplanes lay scattered about the tarmac. Embarrassed by the event, the Lebanese government didn't want anyone to see images of the shattered craft. So when I placed my camera on its tripod and aimed it at the missionary pilot, an airport guard stopped me.

"No pictures of bombed airplanes," he ordered.

I nodded and smiled, then continued setting up my shot. The guard wasn't convinced. "No pictures of bombed airplanes," he repeated more firmly.

"I know," I said. "But I've fixed it so they won't be seen." When he remained skeptical, I said, "Here, look down into my camera. Do you see any blown-up airplanes in there?" Leaning forward, he peered into the viewfinder of my twin-lens reflex Mamiya. There he saw a small private aircraft with its missionary pilot standing proudly by its wing. Behind the airplane was a blur of color, its fuzziness obscuring the stark reality of the enemy's devastating raid. The guard nodded and gave me a thumbs-up. With a click, I took the picture.

I'd used selective focus to capture the bravery and determination of a missionary pilot while suppressing the ugliness of a never-ending war. By turning the focusing ring on my lens, I'd chosen what I wanted to see and what I didn't.

That's the beauty of God's holy Sabbath. It's a spiritual focusing ring, enabling Christians everywhere to make it clear to friends, neighbors, business associates, and family members that they take God and His law seriously. One day each week they concentrate on the splendor of His holiness while choosing to obscure the unpleasant realities in the background of their lives.

God invites us all to begin making beautiful images using the focusing power of His blessed Sabbath day.

Landowner

The earth is the Lord's, and everything in it, the world,
and all who live in it; for he founded it upon the seas
and established it upon the waters. Psalm 24:1, NIV.

I have a deed to it, but it's not mine. I can show you the bill of sale, but it belongs to someone else. My receipt indicates who purchased it, not who owns it.

I remember the first time I walked onto a little four-acre plot of West Virginia hillside as its owner. My wife and I had spent the morning at a real estate office signing the stacks of legal documents that lawyers kept jamming under our noses. We'd written checks—*lots* of checks—transferring funds from this account to that account and making sure everyone who should be paid was paid. We were greatly excited. For the first time in our married life we were going to own property.

After all the formal duties had ended, we shook hands with the satisfied sellers, slipped the ownership documents into our briefcase, waved goodbye, and headed straight to our newly purchased piece of America. Parking the car under the big pine tree guarding the highest point of the gently sloping plot of land—a spot where we'd picnicked and dreamed for months—we got out and walked on soil that belonged to us.

I reached down and plucked some stalks of field grass. "Hey, honey," I called, barely able to contain my emotions, "this is *our* grass. And that's *our* tree, and *our* rock." I motioned to the right. "See those woods? Ours!"

My wife beamed. We'd worked hard and saved long for that moment. In fact, we'd already chosen which house we were going to build on the spot. Now we could call the contractor and tell him to start digging the footers. The land was ours. The dream had come true.

Then a sudden, strange feeling came over me, a feeling of unworthiness. Yes, I owned that big pine tree, but I didn't know how it grew. The field grasses didn't need me to make them green. Even the rocks jutting from the West Virginia soil hadn't required my presence as, for thousands of years, the wind, the rain, and the seasons had shaped them.

It was my land, but it wasn't.

Then I understood. From that moment on, it was my job simply to *care* for my property, to protect it, nurture it, keep it beautiful.

Hand in hand, my wife and I walked among the thick tree trunks and gazed out over the little valley to the gentle ridge rising beyond the distant farm. We felt very close to God. Both of us knew that we'd just become partners with Him in a project He'd launched thousands of years ago. Prior to that time we'd lived our lives as renters to other human beings. Now, through God's blessings and our hard work, we'd become stewards of the Creator Himself.

The Bible makes it extremely clear who owns what in our world. In a word—God. Everything is His, including our bodies. We certainly didn't create ourselves. Neither of us had any part in bringing us into this world. God alone set the events leading to our existence in motion. He declared His love to humanity by making our ancestors capable of procreation. And it is God who expects us to care for ourselves, for each other, and for the land on which we live. All of us are stewards of what He owns.

I've watched the seasons come and go on my little corner of West Virginia. The property still doesn't need me, but I'm totally satisfied to mow its grasses and prune its trees in service to its true Owner while enjoying life on its peaceful slope. All in all, faithful stewards have it pretty good on our world.

Flight

The life I live in the body, I live by faith in the Son of God,
who loved me and gave himself for me. Galatians 2:20, NIV.

If you'd been on a boat drifting across the English Channel on June 12, 1979, you might have seen a curious sight.

At first you would've heard the sound of approaching engines and soon noticed a small collection of motorboats coming your way. Then, following them like an obedient puppy, skimming slowly just above the waves, you would've been surprised to observe a frail, clear-skinned, high-winged aircraft heading in your direction.

Curiously, you'd notice that none of the rumbling noises reverberating from the procession originated from the majestic plane. Even though it had a large propeller that rotated steadily around and around and around, no engine drove it. As the strange entourage drew closer, you'd be fascinated by the fact that the aircraft did indeed have a source of power, but the engine wasn't made of steel or even rubber. No gas or oil lines fed it through tubes and filters. The motor consisted of muscle, tendons, and blood. The mysterious craft stayed in the air and skimmed over the waves as a result of the efforts of a young man by the name of Bryan Allen who sat pedaling furiously within the confines of his transparent cockpit. On that day you would have witnessed aviation history.

He'd taken off from England several hours before and was now fighting fatigue and freak winds on his way to the coast of France. As he drifted by, you'd see the exertion reflected on the young pilot's face, see his wiry body moving rhythmically, muscles straining, in his all-out effort to stay aloft.

The next day newspapers around the world would herald the news that he'd landed safely on the coast of France, completing the very first pedal-powered flight across the English Channel.

That was many years ago. Why don't we see such airplanes parked in garages or moving majestically through the skies of our hometowns today? The answer is simple. As dramatic as the event may have been, human-powered flight isn't practical. The average person, male or female, can't maintain the necessary energy output for extended flights. In other words, we make pretty good scholars, cooks, lovers, and baseball players. But we make lousy aircraft engines.

Christians sometimes strap on the wings of their own dreams and head out over the waves searching for some distant shore and their 15 minutes of glory. We pedal and pedal and pedal, straining to get from where we are to where we want to be. Sometimes we may even reach a goal or two. Trouble is, when we land, we're far too exhausted to enjoy our accomplishment.

As we're trying to regain our composure, as we're waiting for our overworked muscles to recover and our heart to stop pounding, God greets us with an invitation that sounds better and better after each flight. "Would you like Me to be your engine?" He asks. "Would you like Me to carry you farther, higher, and faster than you can dream?"

If we're wise, we accept the invitation. Tired of living strapped to our own limitations, we invite Christ into our lives, into our homes, into our hearts. That's what a Christian is—someone who has decided that human-powered flight isn't practical.

When we accept the enabling energies offered by the Holy Spirit, we learn something quite amazing. With Him driving our thoughts, our actions, and our dreams, not even the sky can limit us.

Eternal Ecstasy

For this reason a man will leave his father and mother
and be united to his wife, and they will become one flesh. Genesis 2:24, NIV.

The truisms are endless:

Marriage is like a violin. It doesn't work without strings. When the music stops, the strings are still attached.

Even if marriages are made in heaven, humans have to be responsible for their maintenance.

If a man has enough horse sense to treat his wife like a thoroughbred, she'll never turn into an old nag.

Marriage is the relationship of two reasonable human beings who have agreed to abide by each other's intolerabilities.

Christian evangelist Charles Swindoll tells of being married 10 years before he began to value the differences between himself and his wife. "It would irritate me when she didn't view things exactly as I did," he says. "She wasn't argumentative, only expressive of her honest feelings. I took this as a lack of submission and told her so."

Time and time again the evangelist and his life partner would lock horns, until one day God revealed to him the beauty found in Genesis 2:18-25. Here he discovered that women were different from men for a reason. God made them that way. "She wasn't designed to be my echo," Swindoll states. "She was my counterpart, a necessary and needed individual to help me become all God wanted me to be."

Something is being lost in our world today, something beautiful. Marriages break apart at alarming rates. Men and women find themselves forced to endure what many consider to be worse than the death of a spouse—divorce. Fewer and fewer people are willing to take the same view as Charles Swindoll did when it comes to differences in outlooks and opinions.

Consider the other side of the coin as presented by W. R. Maltby in his book *Christ and His Cross* (London: Epworth, 1938):

"A good many years ago I knew a workingman in the north of England whose wife, soon after her marriage, drifted in vicious ways, and went rapidly from bad to worse. He came home one Sunday evening to find, as he had found a dozen times before, that she had gone on a new debauch [perversion]. He knew in what condition she would return after two or three days of a nameless life. He sat down in the cheerless house to look the truth in the face and to find what he must do. The worst had happened too often to leave him much hope for amendment. . . . He made his choice to hold by his wife to the end and to keep a home for her who would not make one for him. Now that a new and terrible meaning had passed into the words 'for better or for worse,' he reaffirmed his marriage vow.

"Later, when someone who knew them both intimately ventured to commiserate with him, he answered, 'Not a word! She is my wife! I loved her when she was a girl in our village, and I shall love her as long as there is breath in my body.'

"She did not mend, and died in his house after some years in a shameful condition, with his hands spread over her in pity and prayer to the last" (pp. 54, 55).

No one said it was going to be easy. Since sin entered the human heart, relationships have remained strained and difficult to maintain. But God calls Christians into a deeper commitment in marriage. "For better or for worse" can become a springboard into a more joyous, fulfilling life here on earth and ultimately lead two souls to the eternal ecstasy of heaven.

The Lamb

He did not enter by means of the blood of goats and calves;
but he entered the Most Holy Place once for all by his own blood,
having obtained eternal redemption. Hebrews 9:12, NIV.

During the centuries between Moses and Christ religious life was in many ways simple. If you had unforgiven sins weighing on your conscience, you went out to your flock, chose a perfectly formed lamb, and headed for the sanctuary or the Temple. In its courtyard the priest on duty would ask you to lay your hands on the animal and confess your wrongdoings. The act symbolically transferred all your sins and guilt to the hapless creature.

Then you went home and the animal stayed behind. You were free from sin. The priest killed the lamb. But the ceremony wasn't finished. The priest then sprinkled the blood from your sacrifice in different places about the Temple, thus transferring again all of your unholy thoughts, selfish deeds, and law-breaking activities from the dead lamb to the sanctuary itself. Then, once a year, on what Scripture calls the Day of Atonement, priests dragged two goats into the Temple. One would be killed as a sacrifice, the other sent into the wilderness to perish there.

The one killed had its blood, now symbolizing everyone's sins of the past year, taken into the Most Holy part of the sanctuary and sprinkled on the "mercy seat"—the top of the sacred ark. Through the solemn act the high priest made "atonement," or reconciliation, for both the people and the Temple. Both were now sin-free. Both were cleansed.

So where was all the sin and guilt now? They had to be somewhere. Sin doesn't just go away.

At this point the high priest took upon himself the year's worth of terrible acts, lustful glances, dishonest business dealings, and all the lying and cheating of the entire nation. He willingly accepted the pollution of the sanctuary and then calmly walked over to the second goat. Laying his hands on the head of that animal, he symbolically transferred the whole mess to it. The Temple staff then led the animal out into the wilderness and released it. The animal would die from the elements.

The ceremony was over. The sanctuary, priests, and people were free from sin and guilt. The strange God-ordained system of sacrifice and blood had "cleansed" them.

Have you performed any sacrifices during the past 12 months? Have you visited your local priest recently? selected any lambs from your flock?

One more question. Have you sinned?

Allow me to present to you the most wonderful, most powerful verse in the entire Bible. Read it slowly so that its meaning sinks deep into your soul. "God made him [Jesus] who had no sin to be sin for us, so that in him we might become the righteousness of God" (2 Corinthians 5:21, NIV).

When Christ died on the cross, He wasn't just someone expiring from terrible wounds. He wasn't just a Creator perishing at the hands of those He'd created. Jesus was the *Lamb* dying for the misdeeds of every sinner.

A respected Christian writer put it this way: "Christ was treated as we deserve, that we might be treated as He deserves. He was condemned for our sins, in which He had no share, that we might be justified by His righteousness, in which we had no share. He suffered the death which was ours, that we might receive the life which was His" *(The Desire of Ages,* p. 25).

Today we have no need for an *earthly* sanctuary or sacrificial service because, when Christ returned to heaven after His resurrection, He took the whole system with Him. No lambs need to be slaughtered, because what that symbolizes has already taken place. We don't need a Temple full of priests, because we have one High Priest who has earned the right to be our sole representative before the universe and the Father.

As God judges us in preparation for inviting us to heaven, Christ can joyfully inter-ject, "Remember, Father, I became sin for them. I took their guilt, paid the penalty for their mistakes, and earned their salvation with My own blood."

For Christ's sake God forgives and pardons. And for Christ's sake God adds our name to the long list of those destined for glory. Christ's sacrifice encourages us to come "boldly unto the throne of grace, that we may obtain mercy and find grace to help in time of need" (Hebrews 4:16).

The Lamb has been slain. The blood sprinkled. Atonement made. We're forgiven.

Solo

Even so, come, Lord Jesus. Revelation 22:20.

I tighten my seat belt and adjust the throttle, feeling strange. He'd always been there sitting by my side, telling me what to do, showing me how to move the controls and adjust the instruments. His voice had served as my guide. Now the only voice I hear in the cockpit is mine, mumbling the items on the checklist as I prepare my airplane for departure.

Fuel pressure. *Check.*

RPMs. *Six hundred.*

Altimeter. *Set to field elevation.*

Flight controls. *Free and correct.*

I glance over at the grassy knoll guarding the approach end of the narrow earthen strip that serves as our community airport. My instructor sits looking up at the clouds, ignoring me. I smile. He doesn't want to make me nervous.

But I am nervous. I've never flown an airplane all by myself.

He'd taught me about wings and winds, thrust and throttles, stalls and spins. We'd fought unstable air and downdrafts, learned communication techniques and traffic patterns. Together we'd practiced takeoffs and landings hour after hour, because I wanted to solo, to earn my wings. I wanted to be a pilot.

"OK, Mills," I say to myself. "Line 'er up. Keep your feet moving on the rudder pedals. Feel the aircraft. Let it talk to you."

Pushing the throttle to the firewall, I feel the small metal-skinned tail-dragger move forward. Do I know enough? Have I learned everything I need? My instructor thinks so. He has faith in me and in his teaching ability.

"It takes two things to fly safely," he'd often said. "A well-maintained aircraft and a thinking pilot."

"I'm thinking, I'm thinking!" I repeat to myself as the lurching and vibrating grows more intense from the aircraft's increasing velocity over the newly mowed meadow grass. All I have on my side is the confidence of my instructor. He believes I can do this even though I've never experienced flight under these exact conditions. But I'm alone and have no one to catch me if I fall.

Twenty, 25, 30. The airspeed indicator reveals how fast we're moving whenever I glance at its glassy face. The needle shakes slightly as if afraid of what's coming.

"You're going to be lighter," the instructor had warned. "You'll be off much quicker without me on board. Be prepared for it."

"I am, I am," I say to no one. My feet dance on the rudder pedals as my right hand manipulates the control stick. The aircraft roars as it bounces, shakes, trembles, swerves, and jolts along the ground—faster and faster. I want to fly. I want to know what it's like to sail alone in the vast sea of air.

There's coming a time of upheaval for this world. I'd like to say that the second advent of Christ won't be a frightening event. But it will be. No Hollywood blockbuster, no special-effects house, no artist armed with a computer or paints, can even come close to replicating that future event. It will be noise and fury, screams and trembling, violence and terror rolling over and over each other in a horrendous wave.

"Steady . . . steady," I tell myself as the actions of the aircraft increase. The world is now a green-and-brown blur. The shriek of the engine fills my ears, blocking out all other sounds. I see the trees at the end of the runway racing toward me. They look so tall—so very tall. Had they suddenly grown? They hadn't seemed so imposing when the instructor was by my side. And my wheels! They're taking a terrible beating. Am I doing something wrong? No! I'm doing exactly what I did before when the instructor was shouting encouragement and advice over the blare of the motor. Hang on, Mills, *hang on!*

The second coming of Christ fills hearts with dread. Millions see Him in the clouds, sitting on a throne, surrounded by angels. Men and women run, shielding their faces, desperately searching for a place to hide. They fear Him, knowing He's sinless and they're not. None of them have prepared for His coming, have accepted His gift of salvation. Each of them has rejected His repeated attempts to substitute His robe of righteousness for their filthy rags woven from meaningless works. All of them have turned deaf ears to His ceaseless words of love and have shouted their defiance of His sovereignty. Most damaging of all, they haven't taken flying lessons for the ultimate journey through the clouds.

I glance at the airspeed indicator. Fifty. Fifty-five. Fifty-seven. With excitement driving my pounding heart, I pull back on the control stick.

Other multitudes also stand before the terrible carnage with smiles lighting their faces. They feel the earth shake and hear the screams. While their hearts race and hands tremble, they're not terrified. No. Instead, they're in awe of the spectacle, in absolute awe of what they're witnessing.

Suddenly they feel themselves rising, rising, rising. The shaking stops. The violent trembling eases. They're floating upward.

The ground loses its grip on my little airplane. I'm being elevated by the wind that's flowing over and under the wings. Higher, higher. The tops of the trees slip by below. The air is like silk, soft and buoyant. I'm flying. I'm flying! My instructor was right. I had nothing to fear, because I knew my craft and I knew myself.

Glancing back, I see him standing on the grassy knoll. He senses my joy and knows he has taught me well.

The saints find Jesus waiting for them, arms opened wide. As an unseen power continues to lift them away from the violence, away from the pain, away from the past, they shout for joy. They're flying. They're flying!

Unwailed

And the dead in Christ shall rise first. 1 Thessalonians 4:16.

Death and taxes are two unavoidables plaguing our lives. We can rant and rave, scream and shout, and pull our hair, but they remain.

Christians pay taxes because Jesus said we should render to Caesar his due. So we grit our teeth, haul out the ol' 1040s and W-4s, and have at it. Death, on the other hand, may bring about an even more intense reaction, as discovered by an early Church Father and orator by the name of Chrysostom. Commenting on the ostentatious public lamentations he observed at Christian funerals, he said: "When I behold the wailings and the groanings over those who have departed this life, the howlings and all the other unseemly behavior, I am ashamed before the heathen and the Jews and heretics who see it, and indeed before all who for this reason laugh us to scorn."

He insisted that such conduct basically nullified his teaching on the resurrection and encouraged pagans to continue in unbelief. "What could be more unseemly," he wrote, "than for a person who professes to be crucified to the world to tear his hair and shriek hysterically in the presence of death?"

In conclusion Chrysostom admonished, "Those who are really worthy of being lamented are the ones who, at the prospect of death, have no faith at all in the resurrection." Driving home his opinion, he added, "May God grant that you all depart this life unwailed."

My father once showed me two burial plots he'd purchased near his Tennessee home—one for Mom, one for himself. They're side by side at the edge of a well-kept cemetery hovered over by trees. Realizing the gravity of the moment, we stood around waiting for someone to say something profound. When that didn't happen, we left.

If Christ's coming doesn't intervene, I'll probably visit those plots again. This time, one or both of my parent's names will be inscribed on stone above them. I'll cry, remembering how much they loved me and how much I loved them. But that's all I'll do. Why? Because my tears will come from loneliness, not anguish or fear. My weeping will serve to remind me of the terribleness of sin, of the suffering we all must endure while we wait for our Lord's return.

I'll know that my parents are but sleeping, waiting with me for His appearing. That's the "blessed hope" of the resurrection, what sustains the heart of every grieving Christian.

John Singleton Copley, one of the great legal minds in British history, wrote, "I know pretty well what evidence is, and I tell you such evidence as that for the resurrection has never broken down yet."

I find great comfort in that fact whenever I stand beside graves that are empty or not.

Fire?

*They marched across the breadth of the earth and surrounded
the camp of God's people, the city he loves.
But fire came down from heaven and devoured them. Revelation 20:9, NIV.*

He got the call while he was at work. The message was short and devastating. "Come quickly. Your house is on fire!"

There wasn't much he could do. By the time the fire trucks arrived at his country home, all that remained was a blackened and smoldering foundation. Everything else had been destroyed. Everything.

A few days later I stopped by the site to see for myself what had happened in that clearing surrounded by towering Georgia hardwoods. The man was my boss. I respected him greatly and felt heartbroken that such a tragedy would strike someone so kind and supportive as he.

Tiny trills of smoke still rose from random piles of debris. The leaves of the trees overhead hung withered and charred, limp testimony to the savage destruction that had taken place below. The only part of the house still standing was a section of a brick entryway and the twisted form of a wood-burning stove. Rooms in the house were no

191

longer defined by walls and doors, but could be identified only by the deciphering of their contents, an almost impossible task.

The metal skeletons of two audio speakers marked the final resting place of the family stereo. A file cabinet, doors hanging open, contents spilled and burned, indicated the location of my friend's study. The twisted remains of a bicycle lay intertwined with a garage door railing and a wheelbarrow. Nearby, a well-stocked freezer had burst open, scattering its winter stash of perishables across what had been a garage floor. A pile of broken dishes marked the kitchen as did a pantry full of canning jars. The pantry was gone, leaving the jars and their contents in broken and burnt array.

Bedsprings identified the bedroom, and out in the middle of the carnage rested the intricate metal design of the inner frame of a piano. Occasionally a stray gust of wind would pick up a page from a charred book and send it fluttering across the lawn as if the words written on it were desperately trying to escape the horrible scene.

Such *total* destruction. How happy I was that my friend and his family had been away from home at the time of the fire. They were safe. The only member who'd witnessed the event sat looking at me from his favorite spot in the driveway. He hadn't barked once since I arrived. I guess he realized he had nothing left to guard.

The Bible says that in the near future a great and terrible fire will sweep across the face of our world. Devouring the homes of people good and bad, it will vaporize the past with its fury, sending into oblivion all traces of the kingdom of darkness. Even Satan himself won't be able to stand against it. And when the smoke clears, evil and all its trappings will be gone forever.

But we'll be safe, lifting praises to our heavenly Father as the world and all its pain and suffering, greed and malice, anger and hopelessness burns to ashes. Fire does far more than destroy. It also cleanses, removing all traces of the past, allowing God's children to rebuild their lives and construct new homes.

Everlasting Loveliness

He who was seated on the throne said,
"I am making everything new!" Revelation 21:5, NIV.

William Dyke had been blind since the age of 10. In spite of his disability, he'd grown to be an intelligent, witty, and handsome young man.

While attending graduate school in England William met the daughter of an English admiral, and the two fell deeply in love, eventually becoming engaged to be married. Even though he'd never seen her, the young man knew he wanted to spend the rest of his life with the girl with the soft voice and tender touch.

A few weeks before the wedding the admiral insisted that the groom-to-be submit to a newly developed treatment for loss of sight. It was experimental but offered a slight chance for success, and the future father-in-law wanted William to have every opportunity to live a normal life with his daughter.

"I'll do this if my wife's face can be the first thing I see," the blind man stated.

Later, at the wedding ceremony, as the bride moved slowly down the aisle, she watched as her father began to unwind the gauze that had been wrapped about the groom's face after the procedure, shielding his eyes. Had the treatment been a success?

Would he still love her when he saw her for the first time? A man wants his wife to be beautiful. Was she comely enough for him, or would he be disappointed if he was finally able to see her?

As the last wrapping of gauze dropped from his eyes, William looked into the face of his new bride for the first time. The church fell silent. All eyes focused on the couple by the altar. Then William spoke. "Oh," he said softly. "You're more beautiful than I ever imagined."

There's coming a time, not too distant from now, when God will usher His children into a new world, a world we've loved but have never seen. Only in imagination have we walked those streets of gold or looked upon those walls of jasper or sat under the shade of the tree of life. Sin has blinded us for centuries, shutting out our promised future with its dark veil of evil. But our blindness is only temporary. We will see again, when the veil is lifted. And the sight that will greet our eyes will be far more beautiful than we ever imagined.

W. A. Criswell, beloved pastor of the First Baptist Church in Dallas, Texas, once had someone ask him, "Will we know each other when we get to heaven?"

His answer should provide Christians everywhere with renewed hope and excitement. He said, "We won't really know each other *until* we get to heaven."

Streets of gold, walls of jasper? Such sights will thrill the hearts of every saint. But the inner loveliness of those who've made the necessary sacrifices, who've stood against the overpowering rush of evil, who've stayed true to their Lord in the face of Satan's wrath, will bring to that holy city the richest beauty of all. In the presence of the Saviour we'll find enough joy to last for eternity. But when we gaze with undimmed eyes into the faces of those who, with us, have made the journey, that's where we'll find heaven's most enduring and everlasting loveliness.

ECHOING GOD'S LOVE WITH *FRUITS OF THE SPIRIT*

FRUITS OF THE SPIRIT

Perfect Echo

But the fruit of the Spirit is love. Galatians 5:22, NIV.

A young woman walked into a fabric shop and made an unusual request. "I'd like to purchase some of your noisiest white material—you know, the kind that rustles when you walk."

The proprietor searched for and found two such bolts of fabric and brought them to the counter for his customer to inspect. She picked up several lengths and shook them gently out in front of her. "Perfect," she said beaming, listening to the crackle of the cloth. "I'll take three yards of this one."

The shop owner's curiosity got the best of him. "Excuse me, miss," he said, "but why do you want cloth that's noisy?"

The woman smiled shyly. "You see, I'm making my wedding gown, and my fiancé is blind. When I walk down the aisle, I want him to know that I'm coming. He'll hear when I arrive at the altar. That way he won't be embarrassed."

When God through the apostle Paul provided a description of what a Spirit-filled Christian would be like in Galatians 5, love topped the list. Love is the very foundation upon which all other attributes rest.

It was love that motivated our Saviour to leave heaven and come to earth to live among us. Love drove Him to Calvary. And it will be love that guides Him back to earth again to save us for eternity.

Jesus was a living, breathing echo of His Father's love for each one of us. Christ's life will forever be an example, a standard by which we can judge how effectively we're echoing the Father's love to others.

What is love?

> "It's silence when your words would hurt.
> It's patience when your neighbor's curt.
> It's deafness when the scandal flows.
> It's thoughtfulness for another's woes.
> It's promptness when stern duty calls.
> It's courage when misfortune falls."
>
> —*Author Unknown*

A 4-year-old girl came stumbling into the kitchen clutching her two favorite dolls, one under each arm. Looking wistfully up at her mother, she said, "Mama, I love them and love them and love them. But they don't love me back."

I wonder if God ever feels that way. "I have loved you with an everlasting love," He says in Jeremiah 31:3 (NIV). "I have drawn you with loving-kindness." But then the prophet Isaiah reminds us that: "He [Christ] is despised and rejected of men; a man of sorrows, and acquainted with grief: and we hid as it were our faces from him; he was despised, and we esteemed him not" (Isaiah 53:3).

God's love is stronger than our hate, more unselfish than our pride, forgiving when all we want is revenge, and able to take endless abuse for the sake of our salvation. When it comes to love, we find its perfect echo in Jesus.

Happiness Is . . .

But the fruit of the Spirit is . . . joy. Galatians 5:22, NIV.

Many years ago a little boy received a priceless possession: his grandfather's gold pocket watch. After the man died, the child treasured the gift even more, keeping it with him always, frequently looking at its time-worn face as a way of reminding him of the kindly expression and gentle manner of the friend he had loved so much.

One day, while playing at his father's ice plant, the watch slipped out of his pocket and became lost amid all the ice and sawdust. The boy searched and searched, becoming frantic. Then he suddenly realized what he had to do if he ever wanted to find the watch. He stopped rushing about and sat extremely still. Minutes passed as his heart slowed to normal, ceasing its incessant pounding in his ears. That's when he heard the soft tick, tick, tick coming from nearby.

It is a beautiful illustration of Paul's second fruit of the Spirit. We don't find joy by searching. It makes itself known when we stop our wild thrashing about in life, when we sit in silence and realize just how blessed we already are.

An English newspaper once asked its readers a question: "Who are the happiest people on earth?" The four prizewinning answers were:

A craftsman or artist whistling over a job well done.

A little child building sand castles.

A mother, after a busy day, bathing her baby.

A doctor who has finished a difficult and dangerous operation, saving a human life.

Interestingly, no millionaires, kings, or company CEOs appear on the list. Riches and rank, no matter how much a person strives for them, don't create happy, joyful lives.

When God suggests that those of us who've allowed the Holy Spirit to take up residence in our hearts will discover joy waiting in the wings, He doesn't attach that emotion to any *thing* we might possess. He says that our minds can't help filling with joy when we realize how valuable we are in the eyes of our heavenly Father.

Victor Hugo said it best when he wrote, "The supreme happiness of life is the conviction that we are loved." Jesus came to our earth to remind us of that priceless fact.

On a cold, foggy day in San Francisco a young man stopped his car midway on the Golden Gate Bridge, stepped out into the blustery wind, walked to the railing, and jumped. Officials found a note resting on the passenger seat of his car. In words filled with meaning for a life that had lost its way, the message said, "Happiness is something to do, someone to love, and something to hope for."

Jesus pleads with each one of us to work for the benefit of others, love our neighbor as ourselves, and forever carry in our hearts the hope of eternal life with Him in heaven. Only when we focus on these things, with help of the indwelling Spirit, will we ever experience true joy.

Absence of Wrath

But the fruit of the Spirit is . . . peace. Galatians 5:22, NIV.

On a gallery wall hung an old oil painting, the title of which took visitors by surprise. In intense colors and vivid contrasts the image depicted a violent storm sending towering ocean waves crashing against jagged rocks. The sky boiled with threatening clouds as streaks of lightning flashed across the horizon.

"How could the artist call this representation of horrible destruction *Peace?*" people asked themselves. Then their eye would catch sight of a tiny scene etched in oil and pigment down in the lower corner of the masterpiece. There, tucked away in the rocks, was a little bird sitting on its nest, totally oblivious to the storm raging all about it.

When God promises peace, He's not describing the conditions that surround our lives. He's indicating what our response can be to those conditions. While storms of sin batter His beloved, He invites us to ignore the tumult and remain safely tucked in the folds of His love.

Peace. The word itself conjures up images of quiet evenings by a crackling fire or the gentle presence of soft summer breezes blowing along a seashore. It's a treasure all have sought but few have found. Why? Because contrary to what the world preaches, peace doesn't come from externals. It rises from within.

For many years the people of Argentina and Chile had been quarreling about their boundaries. Both countries suffered greatly because of the conflict. Concerned citizens begged their leaders to ask King Edward VII of Great Britain to mediate the dispute. He did, and in 1902 the two South American governments signed a treaty ending hostilities.

During the celebration that followed, Senora de Costa, a noblewoman of Argentina, suggested that they create a monument of some sort to commemorate the peace that had finally come to the two warring nations. After receiving an enthusiastic response to her idea, she had a statue of Christ shaped from the very cannons that had been used to strike terror into the hearts of the Chileans. Then she had it carried to the summit of Uspallata Pass and set up at the point where the two countries meet amid perpetual snow.

The dedication ceremony presented the statue to the world as a sign of victory for goodwill. Engraved in Spanish were the words "Sooner shall these mountains crumble into dust than Argentines and Chileans break the peace sworn at the feet of Christ the Redeemer."

When the Holy Spirit takes up residence in the human heart, hostilities cease. Anger flees, hatred ends, and prejudice, pride, and arrogance vanish. In their stead rests the most sought-after treasure our world has ever known. Joy replaces sorrow. And in the absence of wrath, we find peace.

Who Do You Say I Am?

But the fruit of the Spirit is . . . patience. Galatians 5:22, NIV.

A schoolteacher had just finished putting galoshes on all of her first graders—32 pairs in all. Before she walked out into the rain, the little girl who'd been attended to last glanced down at her feet. "You know what, Teacher?" she said. "These aren't my galoshes."

The instructor bent and removed them. Then the child continued. "They are my sister's, and she's letting me wear them this week."

With a weary smile the teacher quietly placed the footwear back on her pupil's little feet.

That's patience.

The Bible brims with stories of individuals who exhibited this rare attribute, but none offered such a vivid illustration as Jesus Himself. Imagine what it would be like to be the Son of God, to hold in Your hand the answers to every problem our world faces, yet discover that no one—*no one*—believes You, even Your closest friends.

It bothered Christ. I don't blame Him for being concerned. After all, He'd left heaven, said goodbye to His Father, and traded riches and honor for dusty paths, biting bugs, and revengeful human beings. I have a feeling this was the focus of His prayer the day one disciple finally came through for Him.

"Once when Jesus was praying in private and his disciples were with him, he asked them, 'Who do the crowds say I am?'

"They replied, 'Some say John the Baptist; others say Elijah; and still others, that one of the prophets of long ago has come back to life'" (Luke 9:18, 19, NIV).

Terrific. You give up heaven, get born as a baby in a sheep shed, grow up with brothers and sisters who think You're a fool, stir up all kinds of controversy among the religious leaders of Your nation, preach until Your voice is hoarse and Your body aches telling everyone who You are and why You've come. And for what? No one believes You! They think You're a ghost, which is strange, because You've made it quite clear to everyone that ghosts do not exist.

I'm sure that about this time Jesus was saying to Himself, "Is it worth it? How long must I deal with these stubborn, hard-hearted people?"

With a sigh Christ turned to the only friends He had, hoping for at least a hint of encouragement. "But what about you?" He asked in verse 20. "Who do you say I am?"

That's when a big, burly voice dominated the little gathering, a voice that said something that should often be heard among God's chosen people everywhere. "You are Christ of God," Peter announced with unrestrained certainty.

Suddenly, it all seemed worthwhile again. Christ's patient presence among the doubters of the world had been rewarded. In joyous relief, Jesus told His disciples, "If anyone would come after me, he must deny himself and take up his cross daily and follow me" (verse 23, NIV).

What's the secret of developing patience in a world addicted to instant gratification? When the Holy Spirit lives in the heart, we deny self and service becomes a priority. It's what saw Jesus through to the cross. And it's what will see us through to the kingdom.

The Tender Scene

But the fruit of the Spirit is . . . kindness. Galatians 5:22, NIV.

L ong ago and far away a little boy demonstrated in a wonderful way the fifth fruit of the Spirit. It happened while my parents were serving as missionaries in Korea.

Five-year-old Bobby needed his tonsils out. They were red and swollen and causing him no end of grief. But the thought of some stranger reaching down into his little throat and cutting away his flesh didn't exactly endear the procedure to his horrified mind. He'd die, and he knew it.

That's when older brother Billy stepped in. Now, Billy had lived two whole years longer than his sibling and felt he owed the younger boy the benefit of his advanced age. So with lifted chin and clenched fists, big brother announced that everything would be just fine! And to demonstrate his confidence in that declaration, he himself would allow the doctor to take his tonsils out at the same time.

Hey, if Billy said it was OK, then it must be OK! Bobby agreed that as long as brother was by his side, he'd go along with the whole idea, as terrible as it may have sounded.

My father remembers the day vividly. "When Dr. Pearson carried Billy from the operating room in his arms," he wrote in his memoirs, "there was a big tear coursing down the boy's white cheek. That was hard on Daddy, who had given permission for his operation when he didn't need it."

It had all been an act! The older child had displayed his bravado to bolster the faith and confidence of the younger while in reality unspoken fears had gripped Billy's heart through it all.

That's what kindness does. It overcomes our personal reservations, our hidden uncertainties, our unspoken fears, and motivates us to put the happiness and well-being of others first.

When we allow the Holy Spirit to call our hearts "home" we're opening up our minds to the needs around us. No longer are we concentrating on our inhibitions or doubts. We're searching the lives of friends, family, and neighbors, trying to discover areas in which we can make a difference, in which we can ease concerns, in which we can shine a little light into personal darkness.

Scripture reveals our heavenly Father. "And God raised us up with Christ and seated us with him in the heavenly realms in Christ Jesus, in order that in the coming ages he might show the incomparable riches of his grace, expressed in his kindness to us in Christ Jesus" (Ephesians 2:6, 7, NIV).

When that doctor carried my brother from the operating room, someone else witnessed the child's incredible act of kindness. I believe that at the windows of heaven, my heavenly Father looked down on the scene and brushed aside an understanding tear of His own.

Be Good

But the fruit of the Spirit is . . . goodness. Galatians 5:22.

A child readies herself for a day of activities with neighborhood friends. As she heads out the back door her mother calls from the kitchen, "Play nice and be good."

"I will," she promises.

Two men contemplate hiring a third for a position in their company. They read and review the qualifications listed on the applicant's résumé. Then one turns to the other. "Yes, but is he any good?"

An older woman speaks in low tones to a favorite niece who is celebrating four months of marriage. After hearing about the schedule conflicts and other domestic adjustments the couple face, the older leans close to the younger and asks, "Is he being good to you?"

Goodness. Seems everyone from loving mothers, company CEOs, to nosy aunts are interested in the subject. They all want to know just how *good* a person's interaction with others, ability to perform duties, or relationship skills might be. Why? Because goodness is a standard by which we judge those things.

God says through Paul that when we invite the Holy Spirit into our hearts, we begin to bear the fruit of goodness. It means that not only do we possess the power to overcome the "badness" generated by sin in our lives, but now, with God's help, we can actually start doing good things.

My wife is good to me. I can think of no other way to describe it. She says good things, does good things, even *thinks* good things! Do I deserve such wonderful treatment? Most of the time, *no!* But that doesn't seem to faze her. She just keeps right on being good to me.

Goodness is loving attitude put into action. Since my wife thinks I'm worth the effort, she reveals that attitude by her words, her smile, her touch, and her actions.

I remember the day we got married. Just after the ceremony, while we were standing out in the lobby of the brand-new Cohutta, Georgia, church accepting the congratulations of a long line of well-wishers, I glanced down at my bride. She was busy shaking hands, accepting compliments, looking beautiful in her long, silk wedding gown, the same gown that my mother had worn when she married my dad.

Suddenly it struck me. She was my responsibility now. I had just told an entire roomful of people and God Himself that I promised to love her and take care of her for the rest of my life. Witnesses had heard it! I had to make good on my word.

We've now been married longer than most people attend school, and I've discovered something incredible. Not only do I love my wife because she's beautiful and talented and makes potpie just the way I like it; I love her because she's good. That fact has made my job very easy.

When we allow the Holy Spirit to fill us with goodness, we make God's job easier too. He doesn't have to spend so much time trying to straighten out the messes in our lives, because we don't have as many as before. Instead He can concentrate on helping us touch the lives of others. We both benefit and enjoy the results and have a much easier time in our relationship.

God says, "Play nice and be good." With the Spirit's help we can respond, "I will."

Staying the Course

But the fruit of the Spirit is . . . faithfulness. Galatians 5:22, NIV.

She's not what you'd consider a beautiful dog with her white, semi-freckled body and black-furred face. Even her name bypasses any attempt at arrogance. Her adopted family simply refers to her as Nikki the Mutt. However, this stray who decided to honor a family in Eagleville, Tennessee, with her presence daily echoes a beautiful Bible truth.

Each morning, when 5-year-old Cory Strawn walks to the corner to catch the school bus, Nikki tags along. And then, no matter what the weather, the dog faithfully follows the bus all the way to school—eight miles away. She trots over farm fields, loops around fishing ponds, hops over fences and railroad tracks, and saunters along the shoulder of several country roads, keeping the bus ever in view.

She greets Cory with a faceful of slobbery kisses when he steps off the bus, escorts him to the front door, then takes up position just out of the way of running feet. Here she waits the rest of the school day for her master's return. She eats when Cory eats, naps when Cory naps.

Finally, when kindergarten lets out, it's back home again with Nikki running along the same paths, only this time in reverse order.

"Wherever Cory's at," the boy's mother tells the many news reporters who come to witness the phenomenon, "that's where the dog is."

Rhonda Holton, assistant principal at Cory's school, offers her academic observation. "Nikki is consistent, dedicated, on time, never tardy."

When asked why the dog acts the way she does, little Cory says Nikki does it "because she loves me and I love her."

Faithfulness has become a rare commodity in our every-person-for-himself or -herself world. Society seems to be looking out for "number one." Self-gratification rules. Even a well-known religion includes a reflection of this philosophy in one of its prayers. The faithful bow and ask God to "bless me and my family and nobody else." It seems to be getting harder and harder to find someone to stand by your side in the face of adversity and strife. "I've got problems of my own," you hear. "Let's just let the lawyers sort everything out."

Then along comes the Christian who has invited the Holy Spirit into his or her life. Suddenly neighbors, friends, and family members know that they have someone in their midst who'll support them when the going gets rough, who'll stick by them, who'll not run away in an effort to protect themselves, who'll jog after the school bus and be there when the day is done.

In Eagleville, Tennessee, Nikki the Mutt stays the course day after day, running eight miles each way to school to be near her best friend Cory. How can we, creatures for whom Christ died, turn our backs on those who need us? In truth, we can't, not when the Holy Spirit has stayed the course with us and waits at our heart's door, ready and willing to serve us faithfully until Jesus comes.

Forgotten Pain

But the fruit of the Spirit is . . . gentleness. Galatians 5:22, NIV.

Her scream could be heard a mile away. We knew she was in trouble, and called our neighbor Richard immediately.

Living next to a working milk farm provides many echoes of God's love, none so powerful as the one we experienced late on a warm summer afternoon several years ago. My wife and I were taking our usual after-work walk when we began hearing an agonizing cry coming from a nearby field. Investigation uncovered a cow very much in labor. But something was wrong. Only the snout and one small hoof of the unborn calf stuck out from the birth canal. It wouldn't have been a problem except the hoof was attached to one of the animal's *rear* legs.

When Richard, the man who owned the farm, arrived, he took one look and knew he had a problem. "Calf's not presenting right," he announced. "Looks like I'm gonna have to help ol' Bessie."

After guiding the struggling animal to the barn, we watched in wonder as the man, with the aid of a son, forced the cow down onto the straw. With all the strength he possessed, our farmer friend pushed the calf back into the mother, then reached into the birth canal with his arm, carefully repositioning the still-unborn baby inside the womb. Once satisfied that things were straightened out, he grabbed a small length of chain and reinserted his arm clear up to his shoulder and looped the chain around the unseen calf's neck. Then he began pulling, feet braced against the mother cow's hindquarters.

All during the procedure the big animal had been bawling fiercely, fighting the pain and unusual handling. Now her screams intensified fourfold. For 10 minutes the man worked—pulling, repositioning, pulling, manipulating the chain, pulling. During those 10 minutes the mother cow writhed in agony, making sounds I'd never heard before. Then, after a mighty tug and earsplitting cry from the mother, the calf flowed out of the birth canal and landed with a soft plop on the straw. Mother, calf, and farmer lay in a wet, tangled mess. All was silent, except for labored breathing from three sets of struggling lungs. Then the big cow lifted her head and turned to where she could see her calf as the farmer backed out of the pen, chain hanging limp from his fist. "Happens all the time," he breathed. "They'll be OK now."

Slowly the mother cow stumbled to her feet and approached the calf. On the straw lay the cause of all her pain, all her misery, all her cries. I wouldn't have blamed the animal if she'd stepped right over the newborn and hurried out to the fields to get away from the object that had forced her to the very edge of death. But the big creature had other thoughts.

She began to lick the calf's face while reassuring him with a chorus of soft, low moos. Nuzzling him, she urged him to stand on his own, then carefully guided him to her udder, all the while treating him as if he were the most important animal on the face of the earth.

The cow was loving the very source of her indescribable pain. Her reaction was not revenge or rejection. It was gentleness—a gentleness so filled with concern and tenderness that it was obvious she had forgotten her pain and suffering. When the Holy Spirit fills a human heart, that person begins to react differently to the anguish forced on him or her by sin. Echoing the love of God, they allow gentleness to serve as their reaction to the pains of life.

Victim of Invention

But the fruit of the Spirit is . . . self-control. Galatians 5:22, NIV.

Sir Robert Watson-Watt, a Scottish scientist, came up with an invention that netted him a $140,000 reward, the highest ever paid for a wartime design. His radar saved countless lives and provided early warning to the pilots of Great Britain, enabling them to defend their country against Nazi air attacks.

Years later Sir Robert was driving through Canada when a police officer arrested him for speeding. The inventor had been caught in a radar trap. Sheepishly he paid his fine, then penned a short poem about his encounter with the law, a poem that should hold a lot of meaning to every Christian. Here's what he wrote:

"Pity Sir Robert Watson-Watt,
Strange target of his radar plot,
And thus, with others I could mention,
A victim of his own invention."

Ever felt that way? If you have, you've fallen into one of Satan's most devious plots.

Sin has a strange way of coming back and biting you—hard. It's like picking up a rattlesnake by the tail. You think you've got everything under control, holding temptation securely in your hands. "This is easy," you tell yourself. "No problem. I'm in charge." Then bang, you're trapped, caught, bitten.

Why? Because you haven't allowed God to hold the snake.

Self-control, the type mentioned in Galatians 5, isn't about you being in charge of your life. It's not about you making decisions, planning your own course through the land mines of sin. Rather, it's about turning everything over to a higher power.

Humanity is extremely good at setting traps for itself. We're continually becoming victims of our own inventions. Anytime we feel that we've got the situation in hand—watch out! We're right where the devil wants us.

When we allow the Holy Spirit access to our hearts, self-control takes on a whole new meaning. It's no longer "I'm watching out for myself now." Instead, filled with supplication and thankfulness, we say, "I'm no longer in control of my life because I've given it over to God. From this moment on, He's the center of my thoughts, He serves as my spiritual guide, He's the standard by which I will judge every decision, every choice, and every plan for my future. I won't make a move without considering the spiritual implications of that action."

When faced with sin, we must develop the self-control necessary to allow God to guide, to instruct, to provide strength to resist. We must stop looking to ourselves, to our own inventions, to fight the devil.

Samuel Johnson once remarked that "'Be yourself!' is about the worst advice you can give to some people." He's right. Those who have the Holy Spirit in their hearts have learned that self-control means that they'd rather "Be like Jesus" and allow self to play only a supporting role in the great drama of life.

Can't Say

"Lord, teach us to pray." Luke 11:1.

It seemed like a strange request. Why would the disciples want to learn how to pray? They'd been taught many prayers since youth, supplications common to all Jews. But here we find Christ's closest followers asking for help with something that should have been second nature to them.

Jesus just nodded and asked the group to gather around. Then He taught them a prayer familiar to all Christians. Called the Lord's Prayer, we hear it often repeated in family worships and religious services around the world.

The next time you utter those beautiful words found in Matthew 6 and Luke 11, consider these insights from an unknown author:

"I can't say 'our' if I live only for myself.

"I can't say 'Father' if I don't endeavor each day to act like His child.

"I can't say 'who art in heaven' if I'm not laying up treasures there.

"I can't say 'hallowed be thy name' if I'm not striving for holiness.

"I can't say 'thy kingdom come' if I'm not doing all in my power to hasten that wonderful event.

"I can't say 'thy will be done' if I'm disobedient to His Word.

"I can't say 'on earth as it is in heaven' if I refuse to serve Him here and now.

"I can't say 'give us this day our daily bread' if I'm dishonest or seeking riches by deception.

"I can't say 'forgive us our debts' if I harbor a single grudge against someone.

"I can't say 'lead us not into temptation' if I deliberately place myself in its path.

"I can't say 'deliver us from evil' if I don't put on the whole armor of God.

"I can't say 'thine is the kingdom' if I don't give the King the loyalty due Him.

"I can't say 'thine is the power' if I fear what men may do.

"I can't say 'thine is the glory' if I'm seeking honor only for myself.

"I can't say 'forever' if the horizon of my life is bounded completely by time."

C. H. Spurgeon once wrote, "Prayer pulls the rope down below and the great bell rings above in the ears of God. Some scarcely stir the bell, for they pray so languidly; others give only an occasional jerk at the rope. But he who communicates with heaven is the man who grasps the rope boldly and pulls continuously with all his might."

Every Christian should learn three things about prayer: how, why, and when. That day, with the disciples gathered about Him, Jesus taught the first. *Why* we pray is up to each one of us, for our lives are all different. And *when?* The apostle Paul filled in the answer with three simple words. In 1 Thessalonians 5:17 he lovingly suggested, "Pray without ceasing."

I think Jesus would have approved.

First, Last, Best

"Whoever wants to become great among you must be your servant,
and whoever wants to be first must be your slave." Matthew 20:26, 27, NIV.

Talk about pushy mothers! In Matthew's Gospel we discover a woman whose husband Jesus had nicknamed "Thunder" coming to see the Saviour with a request. Behind her, following like puppies on a leash, walk James and John, two of Christ's chosen disciples.

"Look," says the woman, "when You set up Your kingdom, how 'bout puttin' my two babies beside You on the throne—You know, one on the right, one on the left. It'll make their father so proud."

Yeah, and it wouldn't exactly hurt her status in the community either.

Jesus thinks for a moment, then a surprising seriousness clouds His face. "You don't know what you are asking," He says in Matthew 20:22. "Can you drink the cup I am going to drink?" (NIV).

Drink? Cup? Absolutely! "We can," chorus the boys with their mother's prodding.

"OK," Jesus says, "you will drink from My cup, but only My Father grants who'll sit where in the kingdom."

James and John don't know it, but they've just condemned themselves to death.

217

What Christ was saying was "If you want to be where I am and go where I'm going, that journey may include a cross."

Being "like" Christ means a whole lot more than doing nice things for people. It could have a much greater impact on our lives. "Drinking from His cup" might entail suffering at the hands of others, being persecuted for believing a certain way, or losing a job or even a spouse, because you refuse to compromise your convictions. Being first in God's kingdom requires a life of servitude to those around us, putting their happiness before ours, letting them take the honor due us, watching as they enjoy the life of a sinner while we struggle to survive until Jesus comes.

It all comes down to love: the love that Jesus demonstrated with His life. Only when we infuse our very existence with His brand of love can we ever hope to share it with others. Here's how one poet put it:

> Love is filling from one's own,
> Another's cup.
> Love is daily laying down
> And taking up;
> A choosing of the stony path
> Through each new day,
> That other feet may tread with ease
> A smoother way.
> Love is not blind, but looks abroad
> Through others' eyes;
> And asks not "Must I give?"
> But "May I sacrifice?"
> Love hides its grief, that other hearts
> And lips may sing;
> And burdened walks, that other lives
> May buoyant wing.
> Hast thou a love like this?
> Within thy soul?
> 'Twill crown thy life with bliss
> When thou dost reach the goal.
> —*Author Unknown*

Jesus studies the faces of James and John, and then smiles. Yes, in the kingdom to come, they'll be first because during the years to follow they'll learn how to be last. They'll discover how to place the eternal needs of others before the earthly desires and dreams in their hearts. First will be last. And heaven will be best of all.

Limited

"Love your neighbor as yourself." Matthew 22:39, NIV.

He always looked tired when he came home from work. I'd wave at him, and he'd wave back. Sometimes I'd say something about the weather and he'd acknowledge my observation, but that was all the communication we ever had.

The man lived in a small handsome home about a mile from mine, off a gravel country road surrounded by pine trees. In the back of his property was a rustic barn. Two beautiful horses stood watch over the pasture and drank deeply from a sparkling pond. If ever there was a man who should have been happy, it was he.

The last time I saw him he had just arrived home from his construction job and was seated on his front porch. As usual, I smiled and waved. He wearily lifted his hand and returned my greeting. Then I walked away, leaving him to rest from his labors.

Three weeks later the police found my neighbor's body in a cheap motel along with that of a young woman. Both had died of shotgun blasts to the head. The police determined that the tired man who'd wearily waved at me from his porch had been the shooter.

The full story soon surfaced. He and his friend had been arrested earlier for drug possession. They'd fled the county, heading into Pennsylvania to escape the law. But drug enforcement agents had tracked them to a sleazy motel in a small town and were moving in, ready to seize the couple and carry them off to jail. But as the officers approached the room, two shots shook the early-morning stillness. Breaking down the door, the agents discovered the gruesome scene. Seems my neighbor had decided to be his own judge and jury. His sentence had been swift and final.

When Jesus stated that we should love our neighbor as ourselves, what did He mean? Did that man die because I didn't love him enough? Could I have stopped the chain of events that eventually led to tragedy?

I believe that when God made His declaration recorded in Matthew 22, He was saying that our love should be evident on all levels of our relationship with others. Every contact, no matter how fleeting, should contain an element of genuine concern and caring. My neighbor and I moved in different worlds. His revolved around drugs, alcohol, and immorality. Mine didn't. He was a lawbreaker. I've always done my best to stay on the good side of the legal system. Yet whenever our paths did cross, there was contact. It may have been only a smile and a wave, but that action grew out of love. He wasn't open to conversations about things eternal, but I could freely invite him to enjoy a beautiful spring day.

Perhaps in time we could have discussed more important issues. Maybe we would have become the type of friends who share the secrets of our hearts. I'll never know. In the predawn hours of a Pennsylvania morning my neighbor took his own life and ended any chance of our relationship growing.

I'll always picture him sitting on his porch, bone-tired from his work. And I'll always be glad that I smiled and waved, loving him the only way I could.

Sacrificing Self

"So in everything, do to others what you would have them do to you,
for this sums up the Law and the Prophets." Matthew 7:12, NIV.

Sure, we want everyone to treat us nicely: giving us first place in line, allowing us to choose the biggest piece of the candy bar, taking our side in every argument, being kind when we're grouchy. "Do unto others," our Christian moms warn us as we're about to seek revenge on a playmate.

But how willing would we be to treat others the way we want to be treated when it involves a rifle butt?

In 1968 the North Koreans seized the *Pueblo,* a United States intelligence-gathering vessel, and held its crew under harsh conditions for a year. In one particular instance, 13 of the men had to sit rigidly around a table for hours. Suddenly the door burst open and a North Korean guard brutally beat the man in the first chair, using the butt of his rifle.

The next day guards again ordered the 13 to sit at attention around the table. Again hours passed. Then the door burst open and the man seated in the first chair once more received a severe beating.

On the third day it happened just as it had before.

The others knew that their friend would not survive another attack, so on the fourth day, when the men were commanded to take their places around the table, another in the group seated himself on the first chair. When the door flew open, the guard automatically beat the new victim senseless. For weeks a new man would step forward each day to sit in that horrible chair, knowing full well what lay ahead.

Here was a group of men who'd learned that doing unto others can mean much more than just giving up the little niceties in life so someone else can enjoy them. It involved far more than taking the lesser portion or forfeiting the better choice. In that room, around that table, keeping the golden rule meant possibly losing your life so someone else could live another day.

Finally the guards gave up in exasperation. They just couldn't seem to beat the life out of such sacrificial love.

Such devotion has graced our planet before. Here's how my favorite Christian writer put it: "The world's Redeemer was treated as we deserve to be treated, in order that we might be treated as He deserved to be treated. He came to our world and took our sins upon His own divine soul, that we might receive His imputed righteousness. He was condemned for our sins, in which He had no share, that we might be justified by His righteousness, in which we had no share" (Ellen G. White, in *Review and Herald,* Mar. 21, 1893).

We find the golden rule hanging from a Roman cross in the form of Jesus Christ.

Show, Don't Tell

"I will show love to the house of Judah;
and I will save them." Hosea 1:7, NIV.

It's an old adage all writers hear. "Don't tell your readers what a character is doing," countless training books and seminars instruct us. *"Show them!"*

Seems such an approach works well in the spiritual realm, too.

A local congregation asked Jim, a church leader, to oversee the evangelism of new people moving into the community. Sun Lee and his family had just arrived penniless and alone as refugees from Vietnam. They needed help immediately.

"First, we've got to get you some food," Jim said, helping the family settle into their small, sparsely furnished apartment. "Then we'll try to find you a good job."

The head of the household nodded and smiled, not knowing what the man was saying. None of the new arrivals spoke English.

Time passed. Sun Lee went to work. The two men tried to communicate with each other, even attempting to learn a few words in the other's language, but progress was slow. Jim longed to tell his friend about Jesus, about how He'd died for the sins of the world, but he just couldn't get the beautiful truths of salvation across without knowing Vietnamese.

One day, after studying the language many weeks, Jim decided to introduce Sun Lee to His Saviour. He tried to explain about God and Jesus, but the more he talked, the more confusing everything seemed to get. Sun Lee would repeat in Vietnamese a little of what Jim said, then try to translate the words into English, but somehow the meaning wasn't getting through.

"I can't do this," Jim moaned, a sad smile creasing his face. "It's just not working. How will I ever reach you?"

Sun Lee thought for a moment, then blurted, "Jim, is Jesus like you? If He like you, I want know Him."

For months Jim had been trying to communicate the gospel through words. But his actions, his kindness and concern for the little family who'd come to a strange new world, had demonstrated in living color and stereo sound the character of Christ. His life had been a sermon, and Sun Lee had been listening, learning, and understanding far more than Jim imagined.

For centuries God had been telling the world about the plan of salvation. While prophets attempted to pass on the truth as they heard it, it had been blocked by human frailties, clouded by human emotions, and constantly altered by human interpretations. Then, one day, the telling ceased. There stood a Man, a perfect Man, who would *show* in no uncertain terms what it was that God had been trying to say.

Christ's life was a living, breathing sermon: the gospel delivered in pure form. Truth fell directly from God's lips to our ears and, to this day, provides a standard by which we must judge all other truths, even those contained in the writings of the prophets.

As any good communicator knows: Show, don't tell.

Love Kitchen

"I tell you: Love your enemies." Matthew 5:44, NIV.

H is soldiers have gassed little children and left their bodies strewn beside those of their parents. Poor people have starved to death while he has built new palaces for himself. Medicines earmarked for the sick of his country have gotten diverted for military use, leaving citizens to languish in the deadly grip of curable diseases. Iraq's Saddam Hussein has been an enemy not only to his own people, but to the world. His reign of terror has left thousands dead, homeless, and orphaned.

Now, read again the text above.

How are we supposed to love the likes of Saddam Hussein? The answer lies as close as your kitchen.

My wife is a great cook. Her leftovers taste better than most people's original creations. I don't know how she does it. My journeys into the culinary arts usually find fulfillment in a cereal box or can of baked beans. To me, the invention of the microwave oven is right up there with the discovery of penicillin and integrated circuits.

I've noticed something interesting about my wife's kitchen. It doesn't have a lot of prepared food lying around. You won't find any boxes of ready-to-eat dinners stuffed in her freezer. Instead, I find bags, cartons, and cans chucked full of ingredients: stuff like flour, sugar, oil, fruits, grains, nuts, beans, and seasonings. From them she makes our meals.

Love is like that. It's not already prepared or prepackaged. Rather, it's a collection of ingredients from which we build whatever response we need to fulfill God's command, even His decree to love our enemies.

So when I think of Saddam Hussein and those like him, I look around in my "love kitchen," searching for something to mix together. I'll need a pretty good dose of restraint, because my initial reaction to such individuals is to blow them up with a smart bomb. Next I add a double portion of acceptance, not of what they're doing, but of who they are. Like it or not, God died for their salvation as well as mine.

Then I add a generous cup of concern. The monsters who prey on humanity need a Saviour too, just as I do. We're all lost and need to be found. Before I heave anything larger than a dirty look in their direction, I'd better deal with whatever beam happens to be lodged in my own vision. Sin is sin. All transgressions of God's law are vile and disgusting to Him.

Finally, I cook the above for a few minutes each day in the oven of prayer, seasoning my supplications with a request for guidance. Love, even for an enemy, demands action. While I might not be able to come face-to-face with the likes of Saddam Hussein, I can preach, teach, write, and witness to those who could become *future* Saddam Husseins.

I'll never love any enemy as I love my wife. But I'll use many of the same elements, just in different mixes and proportions.

Yes, with God's help, I can love even monsters if I choose my ingredients carefully and allow Christ to restock the larder of my heart constantly.

All of Me

*Jesus replied: "Love the Lord your God with all your heart
and with all your soul and with all your mind.
This is the first and greatest commandment." Matthew 22:37, 38, NIV.*

The Franks, Germanic tribes that ruled Europe during the middle of the third century after Christ, were extremely religious people. In spite of the fact that they hacked their neighbors to death, they considered themselves spiritual in nature, sometimes baptizing whole armies at the same time.

If you'd attended one of those mass baptisms along the Rhine River, you'd have noticed something a bit peculiar in the ceremony. As the warriors went down into the water at the command of their priests, each of the fighters would hold their right hand high above their heads, not allowing it to dip under the waves. Why? Because they wanted to be able to say, "Yes, I'm a Christian. I've been baptized as instructed by our Lord. However, this hand, the hand that holds my battle-ax, has never been baptized. It's totally free to be used in conflict!"

Funny how the human mind justifies itself sometimes.

Surprisingly enough, our historical friends have modern-day counterparts. "Yes, I'm going to keep all of the commandments, except this one." "Yes, I promise to love, honor, and cherish you, except in those areas clearly outlined in our prenuptial agreement." "Yes, I'm going to dedicate my life to the cause of God, unless I discover something more interesting or more rewarding to do with my time." "Yes, I'm going to love God as long as doing so doesn't stand in the way of my personal fulfillment."

Seems some still hold their right hands above the baptismal waters.

When Christ repeated the command recorded in Deuteronomy 6, He knew all about the human mind and how it likes to justify the person's actions. He recognized that certain areas of His teaching would naturally attract people. Being kind and loving has rewards. Honesty helps bypass a lot of trouble. Respecting elders, being faithful to your wife, returning an honest tithe all bring about a recognizable degree of satisfaction.

But what about those secret areas, those hidden desires and sins that we all work so hard to overcome? How much easier it is to pick and choose our commitments to God, leaving just enough room for self in the relationship.

"That's not going to do it for Me," Jesus says. "Nope. It's either all or nothing." Why? Because a little bit of self can destroy a whole lot of relationship. God wants us all, and I don't blame Him.

As I write this, my wife is in another room in our house sitting at her sewing machine. I can hear her working through the walls separating us. I don't have to worry about how much of her she's given to me, about the corners of her mind that she's withholding, about how comprehensive her commitment happens to be. She's mine and I'm hers, completely, totally, without even a finger held above the water.

Jesus longs to enjoy just such a relationship with us. At the cross He demonstrated in vivid detail how much of Him He's willing to give. Now is the time for us to decide how much of us we choose to reserve to be with Him eternally in heaven.

ECHOING GOD'S LOVE IN *HISTORY*

HISTORY

Choices

Choose you this day whom ye will serve. Joshua 24:15.

The aircraft wing dips below the horizon as we make our final turn toward the runway. The view from the window reveals the dry heat-tortured land that is Egypt. Except for a ribbon of green following the winding course of the Nile River, desert rules the earth.

I press against the window, searching the bright, barren scene below, trying to catch a glimpse of my destination. How will I feel looking into the face of so much history?

Tires scream as the giant jet makes contact with the runway. Engines roar as our pace slows and we taxi to the terminal gate.

How will it feel?

The ride to the hotel presents a kaleidoscope of unfamiliar sights and sounds. Markets and merchants cram the streets while buyers and beggars vie for attention. The activity seems never-ending. There's no rest, no peace. Only constant movement.

Was it like this when he was alive?

Throwing my suitcase on the bed, I walk to the window. With one motion I pull back the curtain. Below me again is the city. My gaze follows the lines of streets and boulevards forming the fabric of the giant metropolis. Cairo hums its welcome.

Then I see them, out there in the desert. Beyond the reaching arms of the city they stand defiant, ancient, still. The sounds of modern civilization fade away, leaving only the wind and the stones. My eyes have found the purpose for my journey, but my mind cannot fully comprehend the sight. I'm looking back in time, seeing into another world, another life.

As the taxicab speeds out of the city, the years begin to move in reverse. Streets become desert roads. Air-conditioned buildings crumble into crude stone dwellings. Cars and trucks transform themselves into cattle, mules, and camels. And rising up out of the hot desert sands, coming closer year by year, approach the pyramids of Giza.

"Here, you buy this. Good price today. You American? Best price for American!"

A swarm of sellers surrounds me as I step from my time capsule. What are they doing here? Don't they know that it's 5,000 years ago?

"Do you need a guide? I know very much about the pyramids. Let me show you everything!"

The voice belongs to a man dressed in a long white cloak, cloth belt tied loosely about his waist. A white headdress shades his face from the desert sun. His smile is genuine, eyes happy.

"Yes, thank you." I say, staring at the stones towering beside us. "I do need a guide."

"Good, you come with me. I show you everything!"

He ushers me away from the crowd. A young boy leads two tall, lanky camels in our direction. Soon I'm perched high above the sands, swaying back and forth to the slow, steady plodding of the beast. The gentle voice of my guide carries me back again through the centuries. Once more I am caught in the spell of history.

Scenes long past focus in my mind. Thousands of sweating laborers toil endlessly, building stone by stone these monuments to death. The crack of whips, the snap and stretch of rough rope inching through wooden pulleys, sound in the still air. The sun illuminates the scene with harsh, brilliant light.

"We go inside now," my guide announces with a sweep of his hand. With uncertain steps I walk toward the Great Pyramid of Khufu.

The air inside is cool. My eyes, accustomed to the bright light of the desert, see nothing at first. Slowly I sense the walls of a narrow passageway that leads us ever deeper into the bowels of the tomb. The only sound is our footsteps and breathing.

"Guide," I say quietly, not wanting to disturb the spell cast by the silence, "where are you taking me? What's at the end of this passage?"

"You come, you see," he encourages.

We begin to climb a long stairway stretching into the darkness. Higher and higher we ascend toward the very heart of the pyramid.

Then, we're there, standing in a room shaped by cold stone walls.

"This is King's Chamber," the guide says as he grins broadly in the shadowy light offered by the single bare bulb hanging from the ceiling. "Here king is buried." His words echo back through the long narrow passageways.

Suddenly a certain thought takes center stage in my mind. This room, or rather one like it in the distant tombs of Luxor, could have been the final resting place of Moses.

The city surrounds us once again as we speed through the centuries back to today. With a jolt we stop at the entrance of a large imposing building. Above the door a sign announces that it is the National Museum of Antiquities.

"Come. Now we see what was in pyramid."

My guide urges me to hurry up the stairs and leads me through the front doors of the building. Inside I discover the incredible wealth that accompanied past kings to future worlds. Gold was the order of the day: gold thrones, gold dishes, gold chariots. Even burial shrouds had gold hidden in them.

My companion explains that when a king died, people thought he passed over into another world, another kingdom. To meet the demands of his new duties, beautiful and priceless tools for leadership accompanied his body into the tomb. Stockpiles of food and wine waited nearby to satisfy the hunger and thirst of the departed.

A small sign above a doorway catches my eye. It reads simply, "Mummy Room."

We enter and stand before the encased remains of past inhabitants of royal burial places. Kings and noblemen, queens and princesses, all lie still within glass-covered stone coffins.

Row by row we walk, gazing into the faces of people who've been dead for thousands of years.

"Look here." My guide points at a body resting near the center of the room. "This one very interesting."

"Why?" I ask joining him, studying the form. "He looks just like all the other mummies."

My friend smiles and bends low beside me. In a quiet tone he speaks. "This man took the place of Moses in the king's court."

His words, to him a simple fact, astound me. The body lying before us was once a young man, very much alive. And according to my guide, the young man attended school with Moses.

See them together, walking the courts of Pharaoh. Hear them talk of future dreams. But then a new voice speaks to Moses, and he makes a choice. "By faith Moses, when he was come to years, refused to be called the son of Pharaoh's daughter, choosing rather to suffer affliction with the people of God, than to enjoy the pleasures of sin for a season" (Hebrews 11:24, 25).

He had it all! His were the fastest chariots and horses, the most beautiful women, the biggest houses, the brightest future. Yet he listened to that new voice.

Time sweeps on. Moses leads a throng of complaining, angry, dissatisfied Hebrew slaves into the desert. His playmate and friend takes the throne of Egypt. Two leaders, two kingdoms, two gods.

One day commotion fills the palace. What has happened? A cry rises from the servants. "The king is dead; the king is dead!" Wails and moans fill the air. The people gather; great multitudes come to pay homage to their pharaoh. The embalmers prepare and wrap his body for burial. Servants carry golden objects deep into the tomb. Ceremonies last for days, weeks. Finally, with great fanfare and noise, the body is placed in the tomb and the chamber sealed. The king has gone to his reward.

Listen. Footsteps sound on a lonely mountaintop. An old man struggles to the summit. For a long moment he stands looking out over the valley spread beneath his feet. In the wind is a voice, that same voice he heard in Egypt. "This is the land which I sware unto Abraham, unto Isaac, and unto Jacob, saying, I will give it unto thy seed: I have caused thee to see it with thine eyes, but thou shalt not go over thither" (Deuteronomy 34:4). In the quiet of solitude, Moses dies. Angels bury him "in a valley in the land of Moab, over against Beth-peor, but no man knoweth of his sepulchre unto this day" (verse 6).

Pharaoh in his tomb. Moses in his valley. Two leaders at the end of two lives based on choices. The story continues.

Centuries later, on a mountaintop in Judea, three of Christ's disciples, Peter, James, and John, see a curious sight. They observe Jesus talking with two old friends, one named Elias, the other Moses. Yes, Moses. Seems one earthly leader found acceptance and welcome in a new land far beyond the sun the Egyptians worshiped. As an example of future resurrections, Christ dissolved the bonds of earthly death that held Moses to our world and carried him to a new life in heaven.

I gaze long into the face of the ancient king. His reward has been scattered to thieves and curators. His empire is gone. Yet Moses lives on, waiting to be reunited with the people who followed him into the desert.

One Christian writer summed up the life of Moses with these beautiful words: "Though his trials had been great, he had enjoyed special tokens of God's favor; he had obtained a rich experience during the sojourn in the wilderness, in witnessing the manifestations of God's power and glory, and in the communion of His love; he felt that he had made a wise decision in choosing to suffer affliction with the people of God" (Ellen G. White, *Patriarchs and Prophets,* p. 472).

The jet picks up speed. Soon we're climbing away from the desert and the city. In the distance the pyramids wait for another day, another traveler. My mind, finally satisfied, rests in the knowledge of a God who lets a person choose, and rewards each life according to the choices made.

One Word

*Let them praise the name of the Lord: for his name
alone is excellent; his glory is above the earth and heaven. Psalm 148:13.*

One day in North Africa a wireless message arrived from the vast regions of the Sahara. It was short and to the point. Again and again the signal rattled radio receivers in every police and military headquarters for miles around. "Water," the single-word call repeated. "Water."

French authorities suspected it might have originated from three aviators who'd been missing for a number of days. They'd taken off on a long journey and never arrived at their destination. Everyone believed they were dead, swallowed whole by the endless expanse of the Sahara. Now, hope for them renewed.

The authorities quickly organized a search. Men and machines fanned out across the sands. Aircraft groaned into the air. Communication links soon sent a steady stream of information back and forth between headquarters and personnel both on the ground and in the air.

After scouring thousands of miles of dry barren land, someone spotted the missing plane. Once safely rescued, the thankful flyers told how, after much time and agonizing effort, they'd managed to get their radio working. By then, they were suffering from such a delirious thirst that all they could signal was that one repeated word—*water, water, water.*

At times in life all eloquence fails and normal communication with our heavenly Father seems to be severed. Our hearts moan in agony. It happened to Job. "I cry unto thee, and thou dost not hear me: I stand up, and thou regardest me not" (Job 30:20).

Isaiah cried, "For thou hast hid thy face from us, and hast consumed us, because of our iniquities" (Isaiah 64:7).

Christ pleaded, "My God, my God, why hast thou forsaken me?" (Matthew 27:46).

What those of us in like circumstance *don't* see is the sudden scramble of heavenly resources in response to our agonizing call. Angel wings flash as heavenly messengers streak earthward, words of encouragement on their lips. Cosmic conferences convene, support teams organize and begin work, and a communication network quickly forms. Short- and long-term goals develop while God's Spirit takes up residence in our breaking hearts, working to reestablish connection between us and the Creator.

"Trust Me," God says, His message fighting the darkness and the doubts. "I know where you are, and I'm working on a solution to your problem. Don't give up hope. Help is on the way."

All such activity, all of this frenzied movement takes place because we've uttered the single word that brings salvation. In our desperation, in our darkest hour, in our great time of need, we've spoken the name above all names. With all of our remaining strength, we've whispered, "Jesus," and unseen by us, heaven has emptied itself on our behalf.

Going for the Gold

I press toward the mark for the prize of the
high calling of God in Christ Jesus. Philippians 3:14.

Certain images from past Olympic Games have remained with me for years: stoic-faced gymnasts and wiry springboard divers twisting in midair, distance runners straining to gain or hold the lead, horses and riders floating over barriers, and the seemingly anti-gravitational antics of long jumpers.

But one particular oft-repeated scene bothers me every time I see it on my television screen. It's the heartbreaking sobs of those who didn't finish as well as they'd planned. Some of the weeping athletes were barely into their teens. Whatever happened to the old "it's how you play the game" ideal that used to lift the spirits of would-be competitors around the world? For some participants at these televised games, you either take home the gold or slink back to your country in shame. One young figure skater from Asia actually apologized to her nation for missing first place by a whole fraction of a point!

Maybe it's because I'm not a competitor. My greatest track and field challenge is mowing the lawn. Water sports for me usually involve a plumber's friend. If I attempted just one of the routines so beautifully executed by the nimble gymnasts who bounce and weave across the floor, I'd break some vital part of my body.

The sober truth is that life isn't about winning. It's about losing. Rarely do we get to wear a gold medallion around our neck. Seldom do we get to look down from some lofty perch at fellow competitors as someone plays our national anthem over the loudspeakers. We get passed over for promotions. Our car breaks down during a Monday morning race to work. Our marriage fails right along with our stock portfolio. One day we wake up and discover that we have sacrificed our most cherished dreams on the altar of practicality. Then our hearts break anew as we watch our children struggle with the painful events pressing against their own lives.

Go for the gold? Of course! Race to win? Certainly. But the wise man and woman, the levelheaded boy or girl, soon comes to grips with the glorious realization that heaven will welcome *all* participants no matter how they placed. In God's eyes, just showing up counts!

One particular winter Olympic Game highlighted a bobsled team from Jamaica. That's right, Jamaica! I sat and watched their beaming faces as they competed, hurling themselves and their sleek, streamlined vehicle down the icy shoot time and time again. It soon became evident that they hadn't come to win. They knew better. No, they'd come to compete, to fling themselves into their chosen sport for the pure, unadulterated joy they experienced from zipping down a channel of ice at breakneck speeds. Their happiness was contagious, even affecting the other teams.

At the end of life you and I may have to settle not for golden medallions, but for golden streets. Not a bad reward for winners and losers alike.

Human Sacrifice

*The things which the Gentiles sacrifice, they sacrifice
to devils, and not to God. 1 Corinthians 10:20.*

I t's an entire city carved out of solid stone," my friend enthused, trying to entice me
into joining him on a journey from our homes in Beirut, Lebanon, to a treeless, arid
region in southern Jordan. "Place used to be a trading center 400 years before Christ.
Only way to get to it is by horseback. We'll have to ride through narrow gorges and
over mountain trails. You wouldn't want to miss that, would you?"

I frowned, still unconvinced.

"And," he said, leaning closer as if about to reveal a deep, dark secret, "we're going
to climb a mountain and see where they performed human sacrifices."

That did it. Cities of stone, maybe. Human sacrifices? Hey, I'm as morbid as the
next guy.

After a short airline flight followed by a not-so-short automobile trip from Amman,
Jordan, through a featureless desert, we arrived in the vicinity of our goal. Sure enough,
horses waited, their handlers eager to do business with visiting foreigners. We rode deep into
mountainous terrain, following ancient paths that wound through weatherworn landscapes.

Then suddenly we saw it, the so-called treasury building guarding the entrance to the city of Petra. We gazed up at towering facades carved into mountain cliffs. Temples, government buildings, marketplaces, countless tombs—all had been skillfully dug out of solid rock.

After dismounting, we explored the valley, enjoying the cool recesses of the caves that at one time had housed both the living and dead of an ancient civilization. That afternoon we climbed high over the valley, finally reaching a flat mountaintop on which rested an altar unlike any I'd ever seen. We could clearly see well-worn chips in the stone where ax blades had struck after slicing through the necks and bodies of thousands of Petra's four- and even two-legged sacrifices. A channel built into the base of the altar served to channel the hapless victim's flow of blood.

Human sacrifice. Is that what God requires of us to gain entry into heaven? Surprisingly, the answer is *yes*. But don't look for altars of stone on which to spill your blood. Don't search for priests in long robes carrying sharp knives surrounded by the wailing, terrified victims of ignorance and misunderstanding. Look instead for a long-ago cross. That's where you'll discover the only human sacrifice in history that mattered. It's where you'll find your pathway to glory. There you'll find Jesus.

As evening shadows crept across the valley, shrouding the city and its painful past in darkness, I wondered if we've learned anything during the past two millennia. Or do we still believe Satan when he insists that *our* actions somehow assure salvation?

On a mountaintop overlooking Petra, humans sacrificed themselves in an effort to appease their god. Near Jerusalem the only true God sacrificed Himself to save humanity.

Beyond the Limits

For I am persuaded, that neither death, nor life, nor angels,
nor principalities, nor powers, nor things present, nor things to come,
nor height, nor depth, nor any other creature, shall be able to separate
us from the love of God, which is in Christ Jesus our Lord. Romans 8:38, 39.

One day a mysterious object washed up on the shores of the Falkland Islands. A passerby spotted it bobbing in the water and plucked it from the waves. It was a large book filled with handwritten notations in a strange language.

The man carried the waterlogged volume to a Scotsman who lived nearby and asked if he had any idea what the book was. "Yes, I do," the man said, carefully turning the pages. "This is a ship's log."

"What ship?" the finder wanted to know.

The Scotsman studied the entries, then gasped. "It's the *Copenhagen*," he said in disbelief. Six years earlier an oceangoing vessel by that name had vanished after leaving its home port in Denmark. The people of that country, especially the parents and relatives of those on board, had talked mournfully of the mysterious, never-explained disappearance.

The *Copenhagen* had been a fine sailing ship, a five-masted naval training vessel.

When last seen, it had been carrying 45 young Danish cadets who were using it to polish their navigational skills. After departing Buenos Aires bound for Cape Town, the ship and all on board had disappeared without a trace.

The entries in the log told of a terrific gale that had blown the sailing ship far off course, sending it southward. Before long, icebergs began to appear.

"They are like ranges of mountains all around us," the writer had noted with trembling hands. "All we can see is white." Another entry announced: "We have abandoned ship. We saw from the distance how the *Copenhagen* was crushed between two icebergs."

The Scotsman turned a few more pages, then paused, his face grim and sad. Pointing at the very last notation in the log, he read: "In front of us the wide ocean is covered with bergs. It is snowing, and a gale blows. Everything convinces me that the sea has taken us beyond the limits of this world."

In one sense he was right.

It is a journey that countless millions have taken, a journey beyond the limits, beyond human reason and hope, beyond, it seems, the very reach of God.

However, the Bible paints a different picture of such voyages. In no uncertain terms it defuses the myth that we can ever travel out of God's sight. Though gales lash our lives, though sorrows bury us in darkness, we're never more than a prayer away from the very real, very powerful presence of the Saviour.

Sin may have its way for a moment. Our lives may end. But we needn't fear even death. It, like the storms that ravish our lives, is only temporary. There will come another dawn, another day, another life. Far from home? Maybe. Beyond the limits? Never!

Genocide

The thief cometh not, but for to steal, and to kill, and to destroy: I am come that they might have life, and that they might have it more abundantly. John 10:10.

Tucked away on a street not far from the grand monuments of Washington, D.C., is a place of horror. The facade of the structure regards you coldly as you approach and welcomes you into a world of sterile brick and iron. No warmth radiates from its windows. No pleasant sounds echo along its hallways.

You've already toured Union Station, the Air and Space Museum, and the rest of the Smithsonian museums. Now it's time to pay homage to those who faced genocide on unprecedented levels. You're about to spend some time at the United States Holocaust Memorial Museum. It will change you.

Before you enter the elevator that will carry you to the fourth floor where your journey will begin, you're handed an identification card. The booklet contains the picture and story of a Holocaust victim or survivor.

My journal highlighted the life of a Mr. Max Diamant, a Vienna-born member of a Jewish family. When he was small, his family moved to Przemysl, an urban center in southeastern Poland where many Jews lived and worked. His parents ran a small grocery store and cafeteria to support themselves and their five children.

On a bright sunny day, September 14, 1939, German warplanes appeared overhead and started strafing the streets. Poland fell quickly, leaving the country under a reign of absolute terror. I'll let Max continue the story as recorded in his identification card.

"We were lined up with Germans aiming their guns at us. Then an officer ran up: 'We need fat Jewish people for soap!' So instead of being shot, we were put on a train. Wanting to die, I decided to throw myself off the train. Others helped me, pushing me through the window headfirst. But when I saw the churning wheels I couldn't do it. So I hung out of the window feet first and jumped. Skidding in the snow, I hit a post that tore a hole in my shoulder. I walked back to Przemysl."

After three years of hiding, Max, along with his country, was liberated by the Soviet army in 1945. Later he immigrated to the United States and became a dentist. He was one of the lucky ones. The Nazis gassed, shot, tortured, and hung Jews and other "enemies of the state" all in the name of "purifying" the world. The Holocaust Memorial Museum tells of those years in heart-rending detail.

Anyone who doubts that an evil power exists in our world should spend some time in that building, gazing at the photographs, listening to the interviews, letting the horror of genocide sink into the soul. And those who doubt that a *divine* power exists in the world should experience what it feels like to leave that place and walk back out into the sunshine of the everyday world.

A powerful evil was defeated in Germany, Poland, and throughout Europe in 1945. Max Diamant is a dentist. The gas chambers and killing fields that ruled his childhood are now silent. God is very real.

Empty Tomb

Part 1

*And when Joseph had taken the body, he wrapped it in a clean linen cloth, and laid it
in his own new tomb, which he had hewn out in the rock: and he rolled
a great stone to the door of the sepulchre, and departed. Matthew 27:59, 60.*

It was a warm, sunny afternoon the day I visited the tomb. I had the whole garden to
myself. No tourists. No locals wandering through. No machine gun-toting soldiers.
Just me and the silent stones.

I sat on a bench listening to the distant roar of the city beyond the high walls surrounding the spot. How should I respond? What emotions should surface? Here I was, a
visitor, gazing into a deep crevice within a weatherworn cliff while life continued unaltered all around me. Didn't anyone else sense the importance of such a place? Weren't they
aware of what might have happened in this garden and how it changed history forever?

Walking to the entrance, I paused, hand resting on the rough face of the tomb. Some
theologians and a few archaeologists believe that He'd been here in this particular spot. They
insist that a long time ago He'd been carried through this opening and placed inside where
it was dark and quiet. Then there'd come the grinding and rumbling of a rolling stone as
the entrance was sealed, shutting out the soft sobs and anguished cries of His friends.

For a moment I felt their sorrow, and it stung my heart. Some were saying goodbye to a Master Teacher. Others had come to bid farewell to a Friend or Healer. One, with unspeakable agony, was whispering final words of love to a firstborn Son. Such sadness!

He'd been their only hope, having spoken of a kingdom to come that would vanquish their enemies and in which peace would reign forever. Now He was gone, and so were their dreams. As they gently laid His body on the stone slab, they silently placed their hopes by its side and sealed the entrance with hands trembling under the burden of broken hearts.

His had been a life of service, bringing joy to whole villages and frustration to those who held to long-treasured traditions. He'd claimed to be God on earth, insisting He was fulfilling ancient prophecies about a Saviour to come. "If you've seen Me, you've seen the Father," He'd told anyone who'd listen. "I am the way, the truth, and the life." Time and time again He'd invited His hearers to turn from their sins. "If I be lifted up, I will draw all to me," He'd announced, indicating that He was the only true avenue to salvation.

So few had listened. They'd wanted immediate release from their enemies—revenge, not revival. Too many had longed for political restoration, not spiritual regeneration. His message had moved too few. Now, even those who'd believed wept the tears of abandonment. The Master was dead. There was nothing beyond the tomb.

Someone else attended the graveside ceremony that late Friday afternoon, a sinister presence lurking unseen amid the garden flowers. For him it was a day of victory, for he'd succeeded in silencing the world's only hope of salvation. Death was his most effective weapon, and he'd been using it for centuries, burying all believers who bowed to the Higher Power proclaimed in Scripture.

Through manipulation of emotions and exploitation of fears, he'd turned minds against the Saviour. He'd created doubts, generated anger, whispered lies. Most had followed his lead. And most had rejected the focus of his attacks.

They'd all gathered, perhaps at the spot where I now stood: the disillusioned disciples, the heartbroken mother, the emotionless soldiers, the unseen presence laughing silently in the shadows. All had said goodbye to a lifeless Saviour wrapped in clean linen. The stone rolled along its track and sealed the tomb just as the sun sank in the west.

Empty Tomb

Part 2

For the angel of the Lord descended from heaven, and came
and rolled back the stone from the door, and sat upon it. Matthew 28:2.

Stepping inside the opening, I waited while my eyes grew accustomed to the darkness. The air was cool and still. Within the tomb all sounds of civilization vanished. There was only calm and the soft pounding of my heart.

Was it like that two days later when the body stirred? Was it like that when the eyes that Satan had sealed in death blinked open in response to the distant call of an angel? Will it be like that someday when I awaken after my own long journey through darkness?

I didn't linger in the enclosure but moved back out into the sunshine. There was nothing more to see inside. Like a castaway shell tumbling in the breakers, the tomb had been abandoned. It or one like it could not hold its occupant. In a blinding flash of light, death had been ordered away, leaving behind a risen Saviour.

What echoes of God's love did I hear that day at a garden tomb? What message did God whisper in my ear on that warm sunny afternoon as I paused at the mouth of the sepulchre and felt its cool breath on my face?

For some, the garden grave holds no value whatsoever. They regard it as only a place of rocks and fables. For others it's simply a short stop on a tour bus's busy schedule.

But for the Christian a garden tomb represents a turning point in the history of the great struggle between Christ and Satan. It's our link to eternity.

Two victories took place at its entrance. Satan claimed the first on a bleak Friday afternoon. But the second victory belongs to us all. When the stone rolled from the tomb early on a Sunday morning long ago, the gates of heaven flew open in preparation for our future homecoming. Satan's most effective weapon, death, had lost its power forever.

Because of the empty tomb, we can live unafraid of the coming darkness.

Because of the empty tomb, we can know that every word, every promise, every invitation that ever flowed from the lips of Jesus is trustworthy and true.

Because of the empty tomb, we have no barriers between us and our home in heaven.

And because of the empty tomb, we can go about our work, our relationships, our lives, and we can survive our sins knowing that our Saviour will never abandon us. Even death couldn't stop Him from loving us.

You may never stand in the silent confines of a tomb near the city of Jerusalem. But the echoes reverberating from that place whisper the same message to us all. Jesus lived, Jesus died, and Jesus lives again. Today the same Saviour who burst from Satan's deadly grip longs to take up permanent residence in your heart and mine.

Ordeal of Spears

*Behold the works of the Lord. . . . He maketh wars to cease unto the end
of the earth; he breaketh the bow, and cutteth the spear in sunder. Psalm 46:8, 9.*

She was only 12 years old and already engaged to marry a mighty warrior. But a fly tainted the ointment of this carefully orchestrated and family approved plan. She said no to it.

Primitive Aborigines living in the bush country of Australia had been arranging marriages for generations. So when a new arrival showed up in the form of a baby girl, suitable husbands bid on the child's hand in marriage. An aging warrior won the right to receive the girl when she reached her twelfth birthday, as was the custom. But on that long-awaited day, the baby now grown into a fine young woman shook her head adamantly. "I will not marry him," she announced. "I don't love him, and that's that."

Her parents commanded, the would-be bridegroom pleaded. The whole village shook their heads and tried to reason with the stubborn child. Nothing would change her mind.

"Very well," the elders sighed with tones of disbelief. "Because of her decision, this girl must undergo the Ordeal of Spears. If she survives, she can have her way."

"Fine," the child said, her voice perhaps a little less resolute. "Anything but this hateful marriage."

Missionary priests from the Keats Port Mission witnessed the spectacle, but were helpless to intervene. The fighting men of the tribe lined up in a row with spears poised at their shoulders. The girl positioned herself 30 paces away and faced the angry warriors. Then, one by one, the men flung their spears at her, sending them sailing through the air with all their might. They were seasoned fighters with strong arms and practiced aims.

The slim girl writhed and ducked, dodged and sidestepped. The first spear missed her. Then the next. And the next.

Finally, all the spears had been thrown except one. The right to fling the last lance belonged to none other than the spurned suitor. The embittered old warrior, veteran of many battles, raised his weapon, and with all the venom of disappointed love, hurled it through the air.

The weapon sailed swift and true, straight for the trembling target. At the last moment, the exhausted, terrified girl pulled herself aside and the spear slammed into the ground behind her. The Ordeal of Spears had ended. The girl had won. Now, at the ripe old age of 12, she was free to marry whomever she pleased.

Modern society may provide more civilized ways to leave a lover, but the story contains a familiar echo. Satan has claimed each one of us as his. He promises riches and glory, fun and adventure. But as Christians, we say no. Then we all face an ordeal much like that of the little girl. The devil lets go with everything he has, weapons of doubt and fear aimed to impale our desire for something better in life. Our task is to duck, dodge, and sidestep his relentless attacks continually.

Our reward? Eventual freedom from evil and a union with the Saviour of humanity. Until that day, keep moving. Satan is a determined suitor!

Turnabout

Vengeance is mine; I will repay, saith the Lord. Therefore
if thine enemy hunger, feed him. Romans 12:19, 20.

A story tells of a Chinese family with a problem.

The Tangs could trace their lineage far into the dim past to a time when their ancestors converted to Christianity. One ancient concept that dominated their lives was: always pay your debts. The family had obeyed the edict faithfully for centuries.

Then a devastating civil war swept through their province, shattering the fortunes of the Tangs. When payment time arrived, they couldn't square their debts with their creditors. The elders and leaders of the family searched for a way out of their dilemma, but could find none. Then they decided on a solution that would save the family's face for future generations to come.

"We are an honorable clan," they announced. "There is only one thing left for us to do."

Somberly the elders of the house of Tang went into seclusion and prepared a beautiful banquet for themselves. The main course? Poison.

As they were sitting down to eat their last meal, gunshots rang out. They heard shouting and several explosions. Then a band of robbers burst into the dining room, weapons poised. "You are all our captives," the leaders shouted. "We're going to hold you for ransom. Your family will pay much for your release."

That's when the uninvited guests saw the wonderful meal spread out on the tables. "Out of our way," they ordered, guns still trained on the elders. Seating themselves, they hungrily attacked the food.

Their enjoyment lasted only a few minutes. Then the hidden poisons began to do their agonizing work. Soon every one of the would-be kidnappers lay dead on the floor.

When the elders of the Tangs called the authorities, they discovered that the price on the heads of the bandits was more than enough to pay off the debts of the entire family.

Satan has been forcing a struggling humanity to sit around a table piled high with what looks like healthy, nourishing food for the soul. Each course appears inviting, smells appetizing, and, for a moment at least, tastes delicious. But his menu conceals hidden dangers, terrible consequences, and heartbreaking disappointment.

However, one day soon Satan himself will consume the hidden poisons. He will experience the eternal death he's been preparing for us all. The New Testament book of Revelation reveals that God and the redeemed will witness the destruction of evil not at a table, but in a lake of fire. The poisons meant for us will eventually cause the permanent destruction of the devil's reign of terror on earth.

And what about us? We'll sit down at another feast, this one prepared by the hand of God Himself. It will contain no hidden poisons. Only life eternal with Him in heaven.

Law of Love

Number 1

"You shall have no other gods before me." Exodus 20:3, NIV.

The sight turned my stomach. A man pulled a heavy cart behind him with ropes attached to sharp hooks digging deep into the skin covering his back. Another stumbled along, barely able to walk, beating himself mercilessly with a whip impregnated with metal barbs and pieces of glass. Still others adorned themselves with fruit hung from fasteners jammed into their bodies.

Why were they doing such horrible things to themselves? To appease the gods they worshiped. They believed that their deities demanded such deeds before they'd forgive the sins they'd committed during the past year.

When God shouted from the top of Mount Sinai, "You should have no other gods before me," He knew full well what other so-called divine beings demanded of their followers. He'd seen the bloodshed, the human sacrifices, the unspeakable pain and suffering extracted from the faithful in the name of worship. The Lord knew how gullible the human mind could be, believing almost anything if the word "god" was convincingly added to whatever teaching was in vogue at the time. Countless millions had lived lives of unreasonable sacrifice and unquenchable fear thinking that, because of their actions, they'd immediately enter a better world when they died, a world that would fulfill every desire of the human heart.

But now from a mountaintop rising above a Middle Eastern desert, the one true God, the Creator of the universe, was trying to set the record straight. He was asking permission to demonstrate to an entire nation that there is only one God worthy of worship and that His relationship to His believers was built on love, not dread.

"Ancient history," you say. "What's that got to do with me? I don't worship golden calves or statues of stone. I know better."

Credit card debts have reached new heights during the past decade. Divorce rates continue to soar, plastic surgeons drive expensive cars, and crime shows no sign of disappearing. Television and radio stations transmit filth, books herald immorality, and lying has become just another business tool instead of a sin. Yes, sacrifices are still being made to some pretty demanding gods.

But somewhere above the din of modern society one can still hear a voice crying out an invitation to reject the gods of the land and to turn our attention to the one Power in the entire universe that can actually save souls. If we listen, we find life eternal. But if we don't, we're following false gods who make us slaves to ourselves.

"Come to me," God says, "all you who are weary and burdened, and I will give you rest" (Matthew 11:28, NIV). That's a God worth listening to—and worth worshiping.

Law of Love

Number 2

"You shall not make for yourself an idol in the form of anything in heaven above or on the earth beneath or in the waters below." Exodus 20:4, NIV.

It looked as if it were going 100 miles an hour even while parked, and I wanted it. That gleaming hunk of metal represented the answer to all my social life ills. No girl in her right mind would ever refuse a date with a guy driving an American Motors Javelin. I'd be the talk of the campus, the envy of every boy in the dorm, the object of respect of all the male teachers in the college.

Such were the ramblings of my young mind as I sat gazing at the vehicle from a distance, not wanting to drive my old red Plymouth any closer for fear of embarrassing the car dealer or chasing away his customers. If Christian communication majors can make idols, that Javelin was mine. I was unabashedly in awe of an automobile.

Time passes. Ten years later I'm digging through the skeletal remains at a junkyard searching for an alternator for the Toyota Corolla my wife and I drive to and from work. I'm knee-deep in abandoned transmissions and small block engines when I see it, sitting alone off to one side, its surface dulled and rusted by the weather, tires torn and flat. It's my beloved Javelin, except it doesn't look like it's traveling at any speed now.

Did God have junkyards in mind when He told a nation of wandering Hebrews that they must not make idols of anything on earth? Probably not at that moment. But He did have the riches of Egypt and the promise of a land flowing with milk and honey very much in His thoughts. He knew how easily sinful human beings can take possessions such as land, gold, silver, and even shiny new cars and turn them into gods. The Lord understood that we as a people tend to worship what we long for, willingly make sacrifices for those things that have no eternal value, and consistently place our affections on worthless treasures. In short, we're weak.

I once had the pleasure of transporting a genuine idol from the Middle East to the United States. A museum of antiquities in Michigan asked me to hand carry a gold leaf-covered statue found by archaeologists digging around an ancient tell (buried city) somewhere in Jordan to a representative in my home state of Tennessee. This I gladly did, eager to have in my possession (at least for a few hours) a real, honest-to-goodness idol, the kind worshiped by millions centuries ago.

As I sat on the airplane, studying the little object held loosely in my hands, I couldn't help chuckling. Had people actually believed that this wooden representation of an ancient deity possessed the power to affect their lives, assure better crops, make them fertile, and improve their standing in the community? What kind of fool would ever fall for such nonsense?

Not me!

Law of Love

Number 3

"You shall not misuse the name of the Lord your God." Exodus 20:7, NIV.

Somebody once figured out that society has created 35 million laws in an attempt to enforce the Ten Commandments. I'm not surprised. Homo sapiens love to make simple things very, very difficult. Take God's third law of love, for instance.

If we're not supposed to use the name of God and Jesus "in vain," as older translations of the Bible insist, why do we find so much cursing and swearing in the media? Perhaps we ourselves have been guilty of blurting out those beautiful words during a fit of anger or frustration.

The answer may lie in a conversation that took place between a general named Horace Porter and his commanding officer, Ulysses S. Grant. One night the two were sitting beside a roaring campfire. All the other men had gone to bed. Horace turned to his famous companion and said, "General Grant, it occurs to me that through all the rough and tumble of army service and frontier life, no one has ever heard you swear. Why is that?"

The leader of the Union army thought for a moment. "I never learned to swear as a boy," he replied. "And when I became a man, I saw the folly of it. I've always noticed, too, that swearing helps to arouse a man's anger. When a man flies into a passion, any adversary who keeps cool always gets the better of him."

General Grant had learned something that God knew all too well when He spoke the above commandment from the summit of Mount Sinai. When a person uses the Lord's name in vain, he or she is creating a dangerous passion in their soul, making themselves vulnerable to the adversary of souls, the devil himself.

Not only that, but by trivializing God's holy name, by turning it into an ugly oath or well-timed comeback, the speaker chooses to ignore the power contained in that name, a power that's very real and very effective.

How we speak God's name reflects our relationship with Him. If we treat it with respect, it's our echo to the world, our signal that we've built an association that has stood the test of time. When we utter His name with reverence, we're setting ourselves apart from the noisy clamor of Hollywood and the decadent banter of the unfulfilled. We're identifying directly with the owner of the name and placing ourselves within the jurisdiction of His power.

Humanity can make laws designed to force citizens to honor the basic tenets of the Ten Commandments, but only a converted heart can teach a mouth to speak God's name with respect and honor. For "out of the abundance of the heart the mouth speaketh" (Matthew 12:34). That day on Sinai God was saying, "Give Me your heart, and I'll teach you how to talk."

Law of Love

Number 4

"Remember the Sabbath day by keeping it holy." Exodus 20:8, NIV.

To a world filled with people dedicated to the task of increasing their bottom line, it doesn't make any sense. Who in their right mind closes their shops, turns off their computers, lets the phones ring, and declines invitations to attend important business functions for an entire day each week? Everyone knows that time is money, the early bird gets the worm, you gotta strike while the iron is hot, and if you don't use it, you lose it!

What was God thinking? The market should dictate when you can take a day off, not some ancient religion.

Then we have the matter of personal happiness. Who wants to sit around all day thinking spiritual thoughts when the big game is on television and there's a sale at the local discount store? Isn't this Sabbath-as-a-holy-day concept getting a little out of hand?

How a person feels about the seventh-day Sabbath doesn't change the fact that it exists and that God had something important in mind when He created it holy.

Many Christians view the Sabbath as nothing more than a business-as-usual day, with one exception: they spend an hour or two at church. While God is thrilled with our worship, He meant for our Sabbath experience to be a lot more than that.

Sabbath is about change. It's about taking time to concentrate on those personal or family matters that we couldn't address during the week. The Sabbath is not supposed to resemble any other day. It's intended to be special.

Whenever I think of Christmas, I remember lighted trees and gift giving. I hear lots of laughter and recall tasty treats from my wife's kitchen.

Thanksgiving brings other distinct sights and sounds to mind. So do Easter, the Fourth of July, Martin Luther King Day, and the most important date of the year, my birthday. Society has created traditions for each of these celebrations in an attempt to make them unlike any other. That's how we honor them. And that's how we can honor God.

Echoes of the fourth commandment reestablish in our minds what the Sabbath *isn't:* it isn't just another workday, it isn't a time to ignore God, it isn't a day to center our thoughts on self. To discover what the Sabbath *is* requires some thought, planning, and creativity on our part.

Nowhere in the Bible does God present a detailed checklist for how to keep the Sabbath holy. He simply says, "The Sabbath was made for man, not man for the Sabbath" (Mark 2:27, NIV). We're free to create our own experience, to discover our own blessings, to enjoy the sacred hours in ways that refresh our souls and strengthen our connection to God. All activities should enhance our relationship with and appreciation for the Saviour. That's how we "keep" Sabbath.

We also need to remember something else. The fourth commandment as well as the other nine aren't "suggestions." They're laws. But like all the laws of love heralded from Sinai's summit, God designed them to benefit us in ways we can't even imagine.

When we remember to keep the Sabbath day holy, it's impossible to forget who created it in the first place. I believe that's the point.

Law of Love

Number 5

"Honor your father and your mother." Exodus 20:12, NIV.

It must have frightened little children half to death. Here was a mighty voice vibrating from the fire and brimstone of a burning mountaintop ordering them to honor Mom and Dad.

What God may have missed in subtlety He more than made up in meaning. As they grew, an entire generation of children remembered the day the earth shook and when the voice of God Himself sounded in their ears. There was no doubt. Parents were to be honored!

The culture of that time regarded moms and dads as far more than caregivers and protectors. God had bestowed upon them a much more meaningful role. They were to represent Him to their children, to act as flesh-and-blood substitutes for His presence. As such, God directed them to live lives worthy of that noble calling, demonstrating daily His consistent and forgiving character.

They were also to symbolize all figures of authority—those men and women, kings and queens, and spiritual and political administrators with whom their children would someday interact. It was a difficult task. But God never said being a parent in a sinful world would be easy.

What echoes of God's love do we hear today in the fifth commandment? Actually, we sense the very same ones that reverberated from Sinai. The parental role hasn't changed, even though society has. God still expects moms and dads to depict Him to new generations. He still depends on parents to teach their offspring the fine art of honoring those placed in authority over them. And just as important, He's telling children to continue to honor their parents in spite of the fact that sin has made such destructive inroads into today's families.

But, you say, what if a parent isn't honorable? The answer is simple. In such cases as child abuse, neglect, or violence, that mother or father has stopped being a representative of God on earth. They've abandoned their role, leaving their sons and daughters to fend for themselves spiritually, to find other substitutes, to discover on their own their way to heaven. It is a dangerous and sad condition in which to place any child.

However, there's still hope for that troubled boy or girl. Jesus said, "I will not leave you as orphans; I will come to you" (John 14:18, NIV). When earthly parents fail in their duties, God offers to step in and make up for the loss.

The echoes found in the fifth commandment are clear. Children have been given the God-ordained responsibility to honor their parents, and parents have received the God-ordained responsibility of being honorable.

Law of Love

Number 6

"You shall not murder." Exodus 20:13, NIV.

Their faces appear daily on the evening news, as do the tightly bagged bodies of their victims. Sometimes they're young. Other times they're old. Their actions have stunned communities, torn apart families, and destroyed the security of us all.

Murderers. Society hates them, God loathes their selfishness, and law enforcement authorities are forever on their trail.

A commandment forbidding murder hardly came as a surprise to the children of Israel. Everyone knew it was against God's law to take another life. Human beings have always regarded this oldest of crimes as a direct violation of everything sacred. But murderers insisted on playing God, making life-and-death decisions on their own. It represented great arrogance and self-regard.

But as usual, even greater meaning hid just beneath the surface of this seemingly simple commandment. It contained other echoes, messages that should continue to reverberate in our hearts today.

Centuries after Sinai, Christ told His followers, "You have heard that it was said to the people long ago, 'Do not murder, and anyone who murders will be subject to judg-

266

ment.' But I tell you that anyone who is angry with his brother will be subject to judg-ment" (Matthew 5:21, NIV). The apostle John added another aspect to the list. He wrote, "Anyone who hates his brother is a murderer, and you know that no murderer has eternal life in him" (1 John 3:15, NIV). Suddenly we find that God's sixth com-mandment includes a lot more than injury to the body. It embraces damage to a person's spirit as well.

When we lead someone into sin, when we corrupt the innocent or contribute to the destruction of their spiritual well-being, we're just as guilty of breaking the sixth com-mandment as the person who wields a knife or fires a gun. God looks at people wholis-tically. To Him, we're much more than a beating heart or a set of breathing lungs. He considers minds and spirits as potential victims too, and demands that we protect them.

What does this say about movie producers who promote violence and immorality in their motion pictures? What should be our attitude toward those who glorify the sinful side of human nature throughout their songs and books? More important, how careful should we become as we interact with others? According to the echoes generated by the sixth commandment, it's possible to commit murder with our gestures, innuendos, and thoughtless words.

But dedicated Christians needn't fear. When we allow Jesus into our hearts, when we give Him complete control of our emotions, when we pattern our lives by His stan-dards, we become life-givers, not life-takers.

How can we know that we've made that transition? One way is by digging through our CD collection, our stack of favorite videos, or the books lining the shelves of our li-brary. If we've refused to allow the murderer of souls to invade our homes and our hearts through what we permit into our minds, we can feel confident that we're attempting, with God's help, to stay on the safe side of the sixth commandment.

Law of Love

Number 7

"You shall not commit adultery." Exodus 20:14.

His large, well-appointed house radiated the rewards of hard work and a keen business sense. In the den sat a brand-new grand piano, while out in the garage late-model cars waited to whisk the family to favorite vacation spots. The backyard boasted a white-tiled swimming pool and attached spa. He had it all, but the evening I arrived for a visit, I found my friend sitting alone, face in hands, fighting back heartbreaking tears.

"She's gone," he whispered. "She's with another man this weekend. Our marriage is over."

It wasn't the first time unfaithfulness had invaded his upper-class home. Before, he'd been the one who'd strayed, but the couple had apparently worked things out. Now their union was falling apart again. The breakup would be permanent.

"They're worthless," my friend said, motioning toward the high-priced possessions crowding what had been the home of their dreams. "Without her, they're worthless."

Since then both have rebuilt their lives with other partners and have learned to live with the pain that destroyed their union and devastated the security of two wonderful children.

Adultery. I've heard men and women say that it's easier to deal with the death of a spouse than face the agony of a broken marriage. That's why God included the seventh commandment in His 10 laws of love. Understanding its effect on the human heart, He knew how much anger, resentment, and bitterness would form deep in the souls of two people who'd once promised to love, honor, and cherish each other until death parted them. Adultery did not form part of His plan for humanity. It came about as a direct result of sin.

The seventh commandment, though short on words, is long on effect. So devastating was it that it became the only condition God would accept as cause for yet another violation of the marriage pact—divorce.

One day, while speaking to the Pharisees, Jesus reiterated the lesson He'd hoped His people had learned at Sinai. But they were still ignoring its truths. He said, "Moses permitted you to divorce your wives because your hearts were hard. But it was not this way from the beginning. I tell you that anyone who divorces his wife, except for marital unfaithfulness, and marries another woman commits adultery" (Matthew 19:8, 9, NIV).

Adultery is one of those sins that affects more than the couple involved. It crushes lives and leaves lifelong scars, disfiguring whole families at a time.

Like many of the diseases modern society faces, prevention is incredibly simple. God says, "Don't do it." It was a powerful command aimed at the children of Israel gathered at the base of Sinai centuries ago. Today it continues to be a powerful echo directed at us. If we listen and take heed, we'll benefit from the deep-rooted blessings found only in true, undefiled love. But if we turn our backs on the command, we're placing ourselves at the mercy of evil.

Law of Love

Number 8

"You shall not steal." Exodus 20:15.

It was more money than I'd ever seen in my life—$1s, $10s, $20s stacked high atop each other, spread across the desk and nearby worktable. Off to one side sat bulging bags of loose change lying open to the sunlight pouring in through the little cabin window.

My father sat behind the desk counting, his lips moving in sync to the bills flipping through his fingers. Even though I was not yet in my teens, I understood the value of money. I knew that in that cabin at that very moment was enough currency to pay off the many financial woes plaguing my dad: the endless school bills, gas and mortgage payments, grocery receipts, even the cost of repairing the old lawn mower. All he had to do was slip a few of those piles into his pockets. Who'd know? Who'd see? I mean, even church-employed conference treasurers had to eat. The large camp meeting crowd that had given the offering during the Sabbath morning service would never be the wiser.

But even as I visualized what all that money could buy, I knew my father would never take any of it for himself no matter how bleak our financial picture. Why? Because of a few grains of sand.

It was a story I loved to hear, one that took place when my dad was much younger than I was the day I sat watching him count money in our camp meeting cabin.

Many years ago, while my father and his family were out for a Sabbath afternoon walk, they passed an empty construction site where little Bobby saw something that brings instant joy to any boy or girl—a huge pile of sand. As his parents and sister slowly continued down the sidewalk, my future parent thrust his fingers and toes into the cool recesses of the pile, carving pretend roads, hills, and valleys among the grains, letting his imagination populate the world he'd created with trucks, houses, barns, and people.

Suddenly reality returned in the form of his mother calling for him to catch up with the rest. Little Bobby obeyed, hurrying after the others with a happy smile on his face. When he reached his mother's side, she glanced down at him and stopped walking. "Bobby," she said, "what's that in your hands?"

The little boy ground his fingers together. "It's just sand," he reported.

"Is that your sand?"

Bobby frowned. "No."

"Then you'd better take it back, because it doesn't belong to you."

My father returned to the construction site while his family waited. At the sandpile he brushed off every particle from his fingers, arms, legs, and feet. Then he rejoined the others, and they continued their walk.

At a very young age my dad had been shown in a simple and beautiful way the true meaning of the eighth commandment. He'd heard its message echoing loud and clear, a message that once reverberated from Sinai's summit. Now, as I sat watching him count pile after pile of money, I knew that every nickel and dime was safe and would get deposited where it belonged—in the church's bank account. I didn't have to ask, but if I had, our conversation would have sounded something like this:

"Dad?"

"Yes?"

"What's that in your hands?"

He'd glance at his fingers and smile knowingly. "This? Oh, this is Someone Else's sand."

Law of Love

Number 9

"You shall not give false testimony against your neighbor." Exodus 20:16, NIV.

A young woman lay on a Florida beach soaking up the warm rays of the sun when a little boy wearing swimming trunks and carrying a towel came up to her. "Do you believe in God?" he asked.

The woman, surprised by the question, replied, "Why, yes, I do."

"Do you go to church every week?"

Again the woman answered, "Yes."

The little boy studied her thoughtfully. "Do you read your Bible and pray every day?"

As before, the woman smiled and said, "Yes." By now he had greatly aroused her curiosity.

After another long pause, the boy sighed and said, with obvious relief, "Will you hold my quarter while I go in swimming?"

Honesty. It's such a rare and valuable commodity in our sin-filled world. Somehow, that little boy had learned that Christians—those who go to church, read their Bible, pray every day—are special people we can trust with something even as precious as one's only quarter.

When God instructed the children of Israel to refrain from giving false testimony against their neighbors, He was basically telling them to stand out from the crowd, to rise above the rest and become known as a people who tell the truth no matter what.

Lying was so easy. It required little work and no amount of commitment. Liars could say anything they wanted to and not have to back up their statements with their actions. But such a practice ran contrary to the high calling of the God who'd offered to lead an entire nation through a desert and into a Promised Land.

God had still another reason for shouting this commandment from the fiery heights of Sinai. His people would always have neighbors. Truthfulness would become a potent witness to those who'd experienced the frustration and mistrust generated by lying lips. Besides protecting themselves internally by being honest with each other, God wanted His people to arm themselves securely with the cloak of trustworthiness. It would build goodwill among those camped along their borders.

Do you hear the echoes reverberating from the ninth commandment into today's world? I'm always amazed when even though a person is caught dead to right in the midst of actually committing a crime, yet they proclaim "Not guilty" when the judge asks them how they plea. They never learned honesty, never learned to back up their actions with their words or how to be a good neighbor.

John Powell once said, "The genius of communication is the ability to be both totally honest and totally kind at the same time."

When God spoke the ninth commandment that day on Sinai, He had in mind that those who followed His wishes, who chose to side themselves with the truth, would communicate in just such a way with everyone they met.

This is still His wish today.

Law of Love

Number 10

"You shall not covet." Exodus 20:17, NIV.

It's a subtle temptation, one that many Christians insist they've conquered. And like the subtleties of its attraction, giving in often leaves no outward evidence of sin. But God isn't looking outward. He's gazing inward.

The children of Israel had just escaped from one of the richest and most powerful nations on the face of the earth. Egypt loved to put on airs. Their temples provided lavish feasts for the wondering eye. The country boasted a caste system distinguished by property and possessions. Money, houses, and expensive trinkets purchased from the never-ending caravans lining the Fertile Crescent marked your station in life, announcing to all who you were and what you would become.

God's chosen nation consisted of nothing more than working-class poor. The descendants of Abraham had struggled to survive in Egypt surrounded by incredible wealth and prosperity. Now a voice boomed from a mountaintop telling them not to covet their neighbor's house, wife, servants, and belongings. From a purely pragmatic standpoint, it seemed He was ordering them to remove a major motivation from their lives—the drive to become more than they were, to own more than they already had, to reach further than circumstances provided.

However, the message of the tenth commandment was far deeper than that. It told the future leaders of God's chosen people to change their priorities, to shift their attention from earthly wealth to divine treasures. God had announced that the Promised Land was a land of milk and honey, a place overflowing with prosperity and possibilities. His people were receiving the opportunity to create their own nation based on God's blessings. What more could they possibly want?

That's where we find echoes for us today. From Sinai's summit God asks us to forget about earthly treasures, forget about keeping up with the Joneses, forget about striving for the newest, brightest, shiniest, fastest, and most popular. He has something even better in mind for His people—for you and me. God's trying to guide our thoughts in the direction of a land flowing with the protein of His promise and the sweetness of His presence. It's a land that we can freely sample here on earth and finally possess in the earth made new.

"Lift your sights," He instructs from within the words of the tenth commandment. "Don't be satisfied with what your neighbor has. I've got better things in store for you now and in the future!"

God is asking us to turn our backs on the subtle sin of covetousness and focus our attention on the not-so-subtle joys of living a life motivated by His Word. Then we can feel free to compliment our neighbors on what they have and offer to share with them the only treasure worth possessing—Jesus Christ.